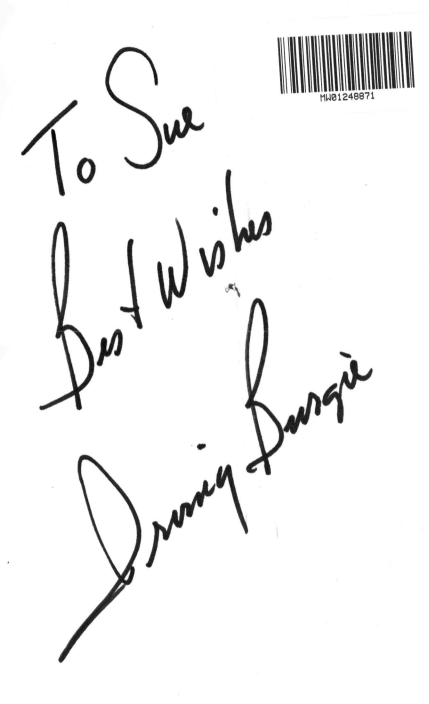

To Sue

Best Wishes

Irving Burgie

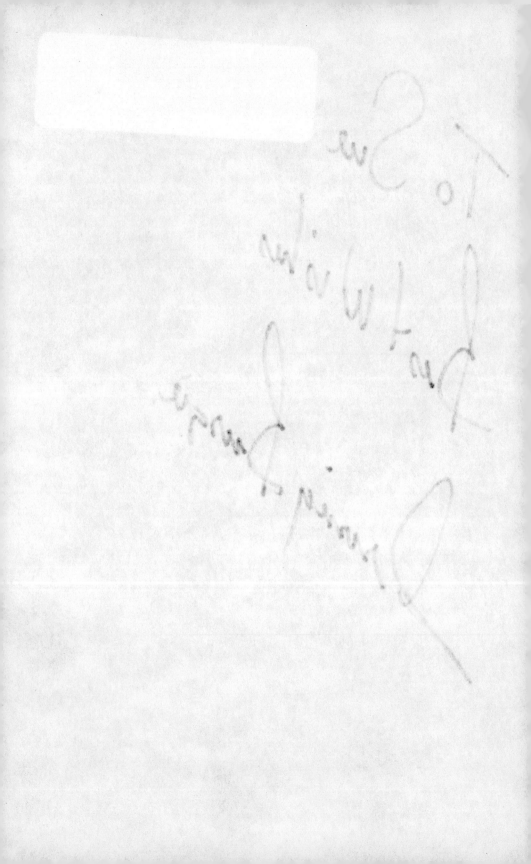

# More Acclaim for Day-O!!!

"Irving Burgie is really someone special. He has not only written a number of major world-wide hit songs, but is probably responsible for the popularity of an entire genre of popular music, Calypso. I had the privilege of knowing Irving during the period in which he created the 'Belafonte Effect.' His songs, occasionally folk based, always had a sparkling originality and brilliance. Eventually, Irving Burgie will be honored and respected for what he is: A Songwriting Giant!"

*—Milt Okun*

"This is a moving personal history of the man whose songs have become a beloved and indelible part of America's music history."

*—Rhoda Karpatkin, President Emeritus,*
*Consumers Union*

"Irving not only opened the world of calypso music and made it accessible to the public; he was also tremendously successful at transforming folk-influenced music into pop culture."

*—Karen Sherry, Senior Vice President, ASCAP*

"Irving Burgie's memoirs reflect his astounding achievements as composer and lyricist of America's most beloved calypso music, set against the background of his fight for racial equality and his dedication to the American principle of individualism."

*—Alvin Deutsch, Esq., McLaughlin & Stern*

"A wonderful journey of struggle . . . and triumph."

*—Abbey Lincoln*

"A sincere milestone and tribute to an era . . ."

*—Rosa Guy*

"The man behind the 1956 calypso explosion . . ."

*—Pete Seeger*

# Day-O!!!

The Autobiography of Irving Burgie

Irving Burgie

Copyright © 2007 by Irving Burgie.

| | | |
|---|---|---|
| Library of Congress Control Number: | | 2006906243 |
| ISBN 10: | Hardcover | 1-4257-2505-8 |
| | Softcover | 1-4257-2504-X |
| ISBN 13: | Hardcover | 978-1-4257-2505-1 |
| | Softcover | 978-1-4257-2504-4 |

This book was printed in the United States of America.

## Song Copyrights

Day-O

Dolly Dawn

Island in the Sun

Jamaica Farewell

To order additional copies of this book, contact:
Xlibris Corporation
1-888-795-4274
www.Xlibris.com
Orders@Xlibris.com
35610

*This book is dedicated to my wife, Vivia.*

*Thank you to my editor, Stanley Brown.*

*I also thank my wife, Vivia, and Stuart Mirsky for their editorial assistance, and my many friends and colleagues who reviewed and commented on the manuscript while it was still in its formative stage.*

.

# CONTENTS

*A New Day*
*Is Coming*
*Every Day*

# PRELUDE

UP THE LINE you could hear it: the thud of mortars, the boom of artillery—and the sounds of war—as American and British troops took on the Japanese and gradually pushed them back out of north Burma so we could build a road. But the war became just more background noise in the jungle, something you just got used to. What I was listening to was a guy in our tent named Jimmy Huston, who was in charge of keeping the company supplied with safe drinking water. He was also an alto sax player who used to sit on his cot and play some beautiful sounds. Jimmy also knew a lot about music theory, at least enough for me. He lent me a book and started to teach me. Pretty soon I was learning about intervals, triads and chords, sharps and flats, and major and minor scales. Not only did it start to make sense to me; it hooked me.

I had never even thought about becoming a musician. I was a black kid from Brooklyn who already had a trade. I was an apprentice bus mechanic who went into the army and got sent to the other side of the world. My job at the Fifth Avenue Coach Co. garage would be waiting for me.

Music had not been a big part of my life as a kid. Like a lot of others, I knew all the songs on the Lucky Strike Hit Parade on the radio on Saturday nights. And I took a few guitar lessons before the war. But that didn't make me a prodigy. I don't think I had any goals that drove me in those days. And not any role models either. Certainly not my father. Looking back a long way, I guess my role model would have been Paul Robeson, the most gifted, talented, accomplished human being of the century, anywhere, any color, maybe in history. But we were not immersed in what came to be called the media. I'm not sure I knew his name or that I even thought about stuff like whom I wanted to be like or what I was going to be.

I sure as hell didn't think my life would be reshaped in huge ways at the end of a gravel road in the Burmese jungle. But that was where it all began.

Whether it was pure chance or an act of God or just relief from the rain and the heat and the boredom, I was on my way to somewhere new, something that would grab me by the soul and thrust me on the way to an amazing, productive and fulfilling life. I accomplished things that everybody who reads this knows about. Even though you have probably never heard or seen my name before, you know my work.

I wrote some 34 songs that made Harry Belafonte world famous and we became just about the most successful artist-writer collaboration in the history of popular music. My songs have been famous for decades. Our first record, *Calypso*, was the first LP to sell more than a million copies. You probably have heard some of my songs a thousand times and still hear them. Even today. Right now, I'll bet, one of my songs—"Day-O," "Jamaica Farewell" ("Down the Way Where the Nights Are Gay") or "Island in the Sun"—is playing somewhere in the world. "Day-O" is used as the hometown fans' cheer in sports stadiums all over America.

# SOLFA 1

*do*

M Y MOTHER, VIOLA Callender, the grand-daughter of a freed slave, traveled from Watts Village, St. George, Barbados, to Brooklyn, New York, in 1917. My father, Louis Burgie, came to Brooklyn from Shipman, a village about 30 miles from Charlottesville, Virginia, a year later. He too, of course, was a descendant of slaves. He had hopped a freight train headed for New York to look for work. They met and married in 1921. They had three children: Evelyn, me, and Will in that order. The family was what a sociologist would label "poor respectable," but with much more accent on the "poor." My mother trained in Barbados as a seamstress. My father was a day laborer. After coming to America, my mother went from chambermaid, to maid, to domestic day worker. My father got a job in a slaughterhouse in Brooklyn. The pay was low, but Daddy often brought tripe home from the slaughterhouse. (Tripe is cow's stomach. It is very chewy.) We ate tripe in just about every form Momma could create, but mostly fried.

We moved a dozen times while I was growing up. We lived in some of the worst tenements, but Momma was always striving to get us out.

For a couple of dollars more we would move to a little better place, and sometimes, we had to move to a place for a couple of dollars less. There was no home relief or welfare in those days; you made it the best way you could on what you had. At times Momma took in roomers, because it was absolutely necessary for the two or three dollars a week it brought in. This extra money went a long way towards paying the 20 or 25 dollars a month rent. A dollar in 1935 was worth about thirty times what it is today and a wage of $15 a week would be equal to maybe $450 today.

The tenements we mostly lived in had tiny apartments, so there were hardly any secrets among the five of us, especially about our financial situation. Not that we children ever suffered or even thought we were living such hard lives. We were no better or worse off than our neighbors and schoolmates. Even so, we heard money talk at home. So we knew that when our father had work, he earned maybe four to five dollars a day and the going wage for a domestic worker was two dollars a day at the bottom of the depression. Obviously things changed for good or bad over the years as our luck and skills and the economy changed. Don't hold me too close to the money; I could provide lots of economic facts and figures, but they would be for a lot bigger economic group than our family, and that's what matters here.

Atlantic Avenue and Fulton Street were two of the main arteries running through our part of Brooklyn from east to west. In our nomadic poverty, we managed to stay in the same neighborhood, even on the same street some time. I still remember three addresses on Fulton Street—1342, 1448, and 1549.

Fulton Street was just two blocks from Atlantic Avenue and both had businesses of all kinds at street level and elevated trains running overhead. Atlantic Avenue was lined with gas stations, tire shops, warehouses and factories and the Long Island Railroad ran above it. There were three Brooklyn stops on the railroad about a mile and a half apart. There were tenements interspersed between the various businesses. Above Fulton Street, the IRT elevated clattered and squeaked through Brooklyn with a station every four or five blocks. The area was densely populated with dwellers living in the tenement apartments at train level and higher, in four—and five-story walkups with entries between stores. These buildings usually had two apartments in the front and one or sometimes two in the rear of each floor. The stair covers were made of cast iron. One day, my eyebrow was split open when I fell on the stairs running away from a drunk we had been taunting.

By the 1930s the whites had moved out of the rundown tenements and blacks replaced them—starting in downtown Brooklyn and moving across steadily over the years to the Brownsville and East New York sections of Brooklyn. The "el" was finally torn down after World War II and was replaced by the A train.

We had no central heating in any of the places we lived in those days. We had a kerosene burner that was kept in the living room to heat that end of the apartment and a smaller one for the bedrooms. The kitchen usually was heated by the cooking and the hot water coil heater. You heated your bath, dish washing, and general cleaning water by lighting that heater. An icebox kept our food cold in the warm weather, and every three or four days the iceman came. You could hear his cry "Iceman, ice" as he rode through the streets on a horse-drawn wagon. In the winter though, we mostly kept the food in a box in the fire escape window.

We moved about 13 times during the Great Depression, all within the radius of a mile or so, usually from one tenement to another, sometimes only three or four months apart, and sometimes only three or four blocks. Most of the tenements were rundown, some were owned by Italians who lived or had stores on the ground floor. The rest of the tenants were poor blacks from the South and a few West Indians. Of all of them, the building at 1342 Fulton Street was by far the roughest place we ever lived.

When I was around ten, I started tagging along with the guys who lived on Fulton Street. I would often "skip the el" (climb over the turnstiles without paying—a nickel for fare was a lot of money) and ride out to Coney Island for a swim. Out at Coney Island, we would go to Bay 9, which was the unofficially designated stretch for us blacks. Nobody told us. We just knew to go there. All we were looking for was a place that felt comfortable and friendly. Of course, the whites (regulars) loved this; if you went to another section, you would be stared at.

We would bring a sandwich from home and maybe buy a Pepsi for a nickel. Hot dogs were a nickel too, if you wanted to splurge. Black kids brought just about everything you could imagine from home to the beach for lunch. One little girl we knew had us in stitches when she pulled out a jar of neck bones and rice for her lunch. If we had our fare to go back home, we usually spent it on a frank or soda and would walk back as far as the Neck Road local station on the other side of Sheepshead Bay, a distance of about four or five miles, and "skip the el" there because the train station was at ground level and easy to sneak onto. But we were happy and carefree and Heaven looked after us because we were both fools and babies.

Most of the people living at 1342 Fulton Street were in desperate straits. Probably all of us were, whether we knew it or not. But we were pretty much sane, except maybe Henry Williamson and his mother. She used to get drunk, stand in front of the building, and cuss-out the neighborhood. I hung out with Henry and a few of the other kids. We played ball and spun cards (the ones that came with chewing gum). My mother had repeatedly warned me about hanging around with Henry but we were all just kids. And Henry just seemed a little more daring than the rest of us.

One day Henry and a couple of us were up on the roof. Henry spied a clothesline full of clothes, which belonged to a desperately poor family in the apartment a couple of floors below. He went down into the yard, climbed a pole, and took most of the clothes off the line. I didn't take the clothes off, but I was there. Henry then proceeded to trample the clothes in the dirt until they looked like rags. Then we went around to the junkyard and got whatever the price was for a pound of rags. Somebody must have seen us, because the story got out. (Kids always think nobody is looking.)

The woman was distraught when she came home and saw much of her laundry gone. My mother got wind of it when she came home from work. When I got home, she called me. I went in with my head down. I finally looked up at Momma and I saw her eyes well up. The tears fell slowly down her cheeks, but she didn't utter a sound. Then she suddenly grabbed me and shouted: "Didn't I tell you to stay away from that boy?" She held a clothesline rope in her hand, pulled me to the bedpost and tied me to it so that this time I couldn't slip away. She then reached for the leather strap and gave me the only real beating I ever got. Even though Momma had just come in from work and was tired, she beat me until she could hardly raise her hand.

After we moved, I bumped into Henry in the street about five years later. He looked very bad. His face looked like it was pushed in. I could scarcely recognize him.

My mother and father slept in the same bed but didn't share much else. Momma was a hard-working, God-fearing, no-nonsense woman, but she didn't make a fetish of religion. She could do some light cussing when provoked, but her children were her whole life. From ever since we could remember, Momma went out to Kings Highway and other neighborhoods that sounded far away to me to do housework. I remember that at one time her rate of pay was a dollar and a half a day and carfare. But even that must have been a lot better than nothing at all for her to make the long trips by trolley car and subway to work for long hours.

When we started school, we went with the door key on a string tied around our necks to get back into the house before Momma came home from work. But she was as kind as she could be to us. We went to the circus once when it came to Brooklyn. We couldn't afford the Big Top, but we went to the side shows, saw things like the Fat Lady and the Frog Boy, ate popcorn, and had a good time. Momma and Daddy also took us to Canarsie and Coney Island and we went on some of the rides.

My mother ran the affairs of the family, and you asked her rather than Daddy, if you wanted to do something or wanted to go somewhere. Though she had a heavy Barbadian accent that she never lost, it was not quite as heavy as my Aunt Meta's. And she was good for an occasional laugh.

My father was a rather quiet man. He went to school in rural Virginia and learned to read and write and that was about it. He told us how they would leave school in those days to pick crops or harvest orchards in season. He was a wiry man of about 140 pounds with excellent muscular definition and the constitution of a horse. He was also quite handsome. When we were small, he worked at Aaron Levy's Slaughterhouse. His pay was only about 25 dollars a week, but he would bring in some meat from work sometimes. Daddy's mother died of consumption when he was a child. He said she was a very handsome woman, who had left him in Virginia and gone to New York to seek her fortune. They shipped her back in a pine box. We had very few relatives on my dad's side, just Uncle Ryan and his wife, Willie (who couldn't read or write) and their two kids, Willie Mae and Vivian, who grew up in Brooklyn with us. Daddy was raised by his uncle in a rural town called Shipman, Virginia, about 30 miles from Charlottesville in the foothills of the Blue Ridge Mountains.

Every Friday and Saturday night he got drunk (a rather common practice among the poor during the Depression). He would cuss and swear at my mother and cavort with his few friends. I remember one Christmas we were decorating the tree, and he playfully threw the whole box of Christmas bulbs on the tree and many of them fell off and broke. But we liked daddy, and he gave us kids a nickel every Friday.

Although we lived in some of the worst buildings, Momma was a stickler for cleanliness. She kept the apartment spick and span and waged a relentless war against mice and roaches. Ritualistically, she would set her mousetrap practically every evening, bait it and empty it in the morning. It was a four-hole mousetrap and sometimes she would catch three or four mice in one night. She would flush the mice down the toilet bowl. A can of J.O. Roach paste was a familiar item in our kitchen. Momma would slice up a white potato and spread the J.O. over the top of eighth-of-an-inch slices and place them in strategic parts of the kitchen. Sometimes when she came home and turned on the light, if she saw a roach, she would hit it with her bare hand, if nothing else were available.

This went on day after day, year after year. My mother washed and ironed our shirts, dresses, pants, and mended our clothes. She was a steady worker and did not believe in idling, even after she came home from a day of cleaning someone else's house.

Besides mixing with the American black scene in the neighborhood, I was exposed to members of my family, who included my mother's sister, Aunt Meta, a staunch and colorful Barbadian, who was always on the lookout for "this generation of vipers and blackguards." Her children were born in Panama where my aunt, uncle, and many other "Bajans" went to work on the Panama Canal, later immigrating to the US where they lived down the street from us on St. Marks Avenue between Franklin and Classon Avenues. A string of first, second, and third cousins, various "aunts" and "uncles," formed a loose network of "family" located usually within walking distance of each other, except for a hifalutin Aunt Sis who lived in Manhattan. Family visitations, West Indian boat rides, bus outings, picnics, and occasional parties were opportunities to keep up with the latest happenings both locally and back home in Barbados. And, from time to time, my mother would send back what small amounts of money she could spare.

Since my mother ran the household, we were strongly influenced by aspects of the culture of the West Indies, sometimes in subtle ways. We were raised mostly on Caribbean-American food. We ate coo-coo (turned cornmeal) and codfish gravy (made from dried codfish), peas and rice, and an occasional piece of sugar cane, all of which could be purchased from local grocers in West Indian neighborhoods.

My mother sometimes baked cakes on the weekends, and we used to marvel at the "miracle" of a checkerboard chocolate cake. Rather than buying them, she also made West Indian coconut bread, cornpone, yellow corn bread, muffins, biscuits, and coconut candy. From the store she bought the bark and made mauby, a bittersweet Barbadian drink, as well as sorrel, and ginger beer. Once in a while she made souse (pig's feet and ears pickled Barbadian style, mixed with cucumbers and served chilled) along with white pudding or black pudding (from grated potatoes darkened with pork blood) stuffed into pork intestines (similar to sausages). When she made a stew or soup, she would top it with corn meal dumplings that were delicious. Sure enough, the main meal on Sundays was usually chicken. For breakfast, we grew up on cocoa, as coffee was never served in the house. Momma and Daddy had tea for breakfast. Evaporated milk was used for cocoa and tea rather than fresh milk. Throughout all the days in all the rundown tenements we lived in, the family never knew a day of hunger. Momma was a very resourceful housekeeper, and always provided a meal on the table.

During the 1930s, many of the poorest parents fed their children tea rather than milk and as a result, their children developed rickets which left them bandy-legged, bow-legged, knock-kneed, and with other signs of malnutrition. But Momma would have none of that, always being certain that we drank an adequate supply of milk.

We were given senna leaf tea on occasion to "regulate the system," as she put it. And in the spring, we got a dose of castor oil as a "purge." To us (I guess to everybody), castor oil was absolutely the worst tasting thing on earth, and there was a lot of grabbing, gagging, and holding the nose to get it into us. Momma would take half of an orange and lay it on the table beside the castor oil, which was "warmed" to make it go down better. We would hold our noses to stop breathing in order to block out the smell and the taste. After Momma poured the tablespoon of castor oil down our throats, she would immediately give us the half of orange to suck on. As you would expect, oranges always tasted like castor oil to me. It was only after I grew up that I began eating oranges voluntarily.

When I was around ten years old, I used to go a half block away to Sheffield Farms, the local dairy, along with some of my friends, and we would steal a few big pieces of ice off the loading platform when the man wasn't looking. We got chased a lot. But we took the ice and sold it for a nickel or a dime to people in the neighborhood.

Once in a while, we got lucky and stole a package or two of milk bottle caps. They were made of heavy waxed cardboard. We would take a one inch square stick about two feet long, nail a rubber band to the front of it, and fix a spring clothespin three-quarters of the way up the stick. We would pull the rubber band back, insert the bottle cap in the rubber band and insert both into the grip end of the clothesline pin. When pressed, the other end of the clothespin would release the rubber band and would send the bottle top spinning forward a considerable distance. Sometimes, we organized "zip gun" wars and spent the day battling with these guns. Fortunately, none of our particular group ever lost an eye or suffered serious injury.

We went fishing too. Not the kind of fishing country boys do, but fishing for money. It happened this way: In 1934, when I lived at 1342 Fulton Street, the new Independent Subway System extended into Brooklyn. The famous A train came to Brooklyn. Sidewalk grates were used for ventilation at subway stations and all kinds of debris and, once in a while, coins fell through the grates.

We went fishing through the grates for the coins. We made our fishing lines from a weight such as a small lock or anything heavy with a flat end that was small enough to fit into the gratings. To the weight we tied a piece of string that was long enough to touch the bottom, which was about 12 feet down. We then diligently and slowly looked for coins as we walked along on top of the gratings. When a nickel, dime, or quarter was spotted, we went into action. To the end of the weight, we would affix a piece of chewing gum, strike a match and put it to the gum (to make it extra sticky), then let down the string with the weight and gum attached through the grate. As we held the string, it would sway back and forth over the coin until our timing told us it was time to drop the gummed weight.

This required some skill—and luck—and if all went well, the weight would land on the coin. Sometimes, it would not land squarely enough and the coin would drop off on its upward journey. Other times, we missed the coin altogether, and would have to pull our line back up to get the debris off the gum and try again. The coin would be drawn slowly up on the string until it reached the grating. We would then put our fingers into the grate beside it, and with some deftness and a little luck, the coin was ours.

This subway grate fishing often attracted several curious passersby who would stop and get involved even to the point of rooting for us. As the coin started upward there would be a shout or cheers; if we were clever enough to get the coin we got shouts of victory and approval.

Besides the sport involved in this type of fishing, kids considered the money well worth going after—a quarter or dime in those days was quite a prize. The subway fare was five cents. A large Mister Goodbar was five cents. A whole Baby Ruth was also five cents (and about twice as big as those sold today for much more). A box of popcorn was five cents and a chocolate Houton bar was two cents. Lollipops were one cent each, as were a variety of loose candies. A big Pepsi Cola, which had just appeared on the market, was twice as big as a Coca Cola and cost five cents, and a half of a pie sold for a nickel. You could go to the movie house around the corner on Saturday before noon for five cents (children) and see seven or eight cartoons, a serial, and the regular three pictures.

In the pre-Depression years of the 1920s when everyone (meaning the blacks living in Brooklyn) was poor, children still skipped rope, played ball, laughed, and had a good time. Practically nothing was based on money. There was never quite enough, but despite the grim times, the family held together—and developed.

I was the second child, coming one year after my sister Evelyn. They say I was an unusually bright youngster (and I won't dispute that characterization). After starting school in the kindergarten, at P.S. 42, the first grade teacher found me so advanced in reading and writing that all I had to do was run errands for her. At the end of that school year, I was skipped from the first to the third grade. There I found myself in the same class as my sister who was a year older.

From then on, I lost interest in schoolwork. My sister always got an A in conduct and I usually got a C or D. She would get a B in schoolwork while I got a C. My worst subject was math, and I never did get the hang of short division or fractions. This was generally the case until the eighth grade when we graduated P.S. 93. My sister went on to Girls High School in Brooklyn and took a commercial course. I went to Brooklyn High School for Metal Trades—a vocational high school, which was in an old factory building on Flatbush Avenue Extension at the foot of the Manhattan Bridge. We mostly had shop-classes because the school was really a sort of "continuation school" for high school dropouts. I needed to go there for my first year of high school while waiting for admission to the newly-constructed Brooklyn High School of Automotive Trades, which would open the following year in Greenpoint. I wasn't much of a student but could read and write better than most and was adept at drawing and drafting.

In the early 1920s, racial discrimination was such an integral part of society that it wasn't even called that. It was more of a condition blacks routinely expected. Except for going to work, most blacks seldom ventured out of their own neighborhoods (or territory as the kids called it). Consequently, overt discrimination was seldom encountered. In our particular case, there were still several white kids at P.S. 93, and this was augmented by a white children's home two blocks from the school on Herkimer Street and Kingston Avenue, which fed scores of children to the school and maintained about a 40-percent white minority there. All the teachers were white; however this did not bother us in the least, as probably only a handful of blacks had the training to qualify as teachers. The immigrant whites—mostly Italians, Greeks, Poles, and Irish—worked in the sweatshops of the garment industry and for the Department of Sanitation and were just one step better off than the blacks, so they had nothing to shout about either.

America was fast gathering the poor and the hungry of the world. Being mostly little more than serfs in their own country, immigrants were happier to be poor in America. America was the land of hope—and a place where a dollar could be made. Outside encouragement for poor black kids, or poor whites for that matter, was practically non-existent. As for me, in spite of the promise I showed early in life, and my obvious gifts, I never heard so much as a mention of the possibility of any of us going to college when we grew up. The only distinctive aspect of my later elementary school years was the two or three occasions in which my mother had to appear at the school for discipline complaints.

After grammar school, I went on to high school. Although not much of a challenge to me, Brooklyn Automotive High School was brand-new and among the best of the vocational schools. During these high school years at Brooklyn Automotive, I was a sensitive, mischievous boy who didn't have much interest in studies and did not go out for any of the school teams. The school was well integrated and blacks made up about 30 percent of the enrollment.

# SOLFA 2

*re*

A S A TEENAGER I managed to stay out of any real trouble and began to read a bit more from the school library. At the age of 13 I could boast about reading D. H. Lawrence's *Lady Chatterley's Lover*, when my mother unwittingly brought it home among a bunch of old books that the woman she worked for had thrown out.

On St. Andrews Place, the bunch of kids I hung out with at about age 12 played all kinds of ball: stickball, punch ball, handball, stoopball, and touch football. Basketball was confined to the schoolyard and was not near as popular then as it is today. It got a little rougher when we played downs, in which blocking was allowed but not tackling. Then a couple of the guys wanted to play real football (rough tackling). There was one guy whose brother was older than we were and he became our coach.

We worked on high-low blocking, running, and passing—not on a field, but right out in the street. A couple of the guys even had helmets but most didn't. Two or three had shoulder pads and some had made pads at home. Everybody wanted to be the quarterback. We got a little

bored with practicing and one day decided to look for a game. There
was no such thing as a league. We walked over to the other side of
Prospect Park to Park Circle where several parks department fields
were laid out, one after the other.

We looked around, and after a while we found a white team that had
just found out the team they were supposed to play against had canceled
out. They wore bright red uniforms fully equipped with helmets, pads,
and all. They hemmed and hawed at first, but I guess they didn't want
to disappoint their players, so they agreed to play us. Man! Those young
white boys were real football players. They were wiping up the field
with us. We were playing mostly without pads or helmets. And they
were tearing us to shreds in the line, and their backfield was running
roughshod over us. They would march to a touchdown almost every time
they got the ball. At first, our backfield was arguing about who was going
to get the ball but as the game progressed, everyone began to pray that
the quarterback would not give the ball to him. After being hit by three
bone-crushing tacklers, one by one the whole backfield chickened out.
The game was finally over when even the quarterback refused to try a
quarterback sneak. So much for our budding football team.

When I was 12 and about to graduate from P.S. 93, my sister and
I got a severe jolt. Our family name was going to be changed. The
family name that we used all through school was Burgie (soft g). My
mother explained to us that my father's name was actually Bowling.
He didn't know who his father was and his mother died when he was
only three or four; he was raised by his mother's sister, along with his
uncle Ryan, who was actually seven years his junior. Their family name
was Buggie. Yes, Buggie, like horse and buggy.

We learned that my father took that name when he joined that family
and my mother was married with it. It was on our birth certificates.
When we started school my mother changed the first g to r in the
spelling of the name, making it Burgie instead of Buggie. The name

Burgie was the only name we knew until we were about to leave grammar school.

I remembered Mickey Rooney, in a movie, boast that he was "free, white, and 21," and I, only a kid of 12, was highly embarrassed and outraged by it. Now here I was, Jim-Crowed, black, and surnamed Buggie! This revelation hit us like a ton of bricks. My mother said she had to go up to the school and have them put Evelyn and Irving Buggie on our diplomas to make them legal for graduation. We begged our mother to give us time to prepare ourselves. My sister and I sat around for the next two evenings pondering our fate. Despite the difficulties and prejudices, we were proud to be black. Despite being poor, we worked hard at keeping ourselves clean and presentable, but this revelation of our legal name at the age of 12 or 13 really devastated us. Why us? we asked.

After much soul searching, one of the explanations that my sister jokingly volunteered was that God wanted to even up the score for turning us out so good-looking. We thought and thought and finally came up with the strategy of introducing ourselves to people as Buggie, that is, Buggie with the soft g sound like budgie. We tried it out between ourselves and it seemed to work. We patted ourselves on the back for being so resourceful and ran and told Momma. She wasn't quite convinced but she told us to try it. We went to school and tried it on a few friends but it was really hard explaining it to them—much harder than we had bargained for—that Buggie was pronounced budgie. But invariably, most of them didn't seem to go for it. They still called us Buggie with the hard g like buggy.

Probably, the most embarrassing time was at the beginning of the term when the teachers would call the roll. They would get to our name, hesitate, look up at the class, and look back at the roll and finally: Buggie? And the class would go up in smoke.

Well, we got quite a razzing from the kids and all through high school the stigma and embarrassment of that name plagued us; we were often the butt of jokes. It really kept us off-balance socially. Just about the time of our high school graduation, my mother went to court to have the family name legally changed to Burgie just before I entered the Army at 18 in 1942.

Sex—the subject was taboo in most homes during my growing up and it was not mentioned in school. Open pornography was banned and even burlesque shows, which were exclusively for adults, came under fire. During the La Guardia administration, Billy Minsky's, the most famous burlesque show in downtown Brooklyn, was closed down and Minsky had to relocate to Chicago. There was a lot of pressure to keep Sally Rand, the famous fan dancer, star of the 1933 Chicago World's Fair, out of the New York World's Fair of 1939 and 1940, but she was finally allowed to perform and became one of the hits at the fair. Nude magazines did not exist and the drawings of near nudes by the illustrator George Petty, which appeared in *Esquire* magazine, were considered daring.

A guy named Nathan in my science class in the seventh and eighth grades, used to bring pocket-size porno comic books to school that featured such characters as Popeye, Betty Boop, Winnie Winkle, and Little Orphan Annie and we would pass them around under the desks to certain classmates to look at during Mr. McMahon's lecture because nobody paid any attention to him anyway.

But sex in general was a pretty "underground" operation when we were growing up. At the age of six, a girl playmate took me down to the cellar, pulled down her panties, pulled me down on top of her, and we sort of rubbed tummies for a while. As I recall, it was an intriguing "secret" adventure.

So there were the five of us in the family: we three children, Momma and Daddy. Most of the places we lived in were railroad flats. These were usually a kitchen, dining room, and two bedrooms, with a toilet at the end of the landing. One room opened into another, with no hallway inside the apartment. When we were growing up, my sister Evelyn and I slept together in one bed. Our parents slept in the other bedroom. My brother Will slept in the crib until he was literally busting out of it, then he joined Evelyn and me. When Evelyn was about six, she got her own bed because Momma felt she was getting too old to be sleeping with us. Some of these apartments had another small room, which was used to rent to roomers. Many a poor family took in a roomer—usually a single man—to supplement the rent, usually somebody just coming into town from Puerto Rico or the Caribbean, looking for a place to stay until he got himself situated. The three or four dollars a week they paid went a long way toward paying our rent. Often there was no separate room for them. Sometimes they slept on a cot or daybed in the dining room.

Our first roomer was Louie Ramos, a handsome, tall Puerto Rican, who spoke only half English. He stayed with us for a couple of months when we lived at 971 St. Marks Avenue. I was about eight years old then. I mainly remember that Louie drank more than his share of whiskey and was a hot number among the ladies in the neighborhood.

From 971 St. Marks, we moved to 1342 Fulton Street, which I remember being very rough. A small Puerto Rican man about 40 named Joe Pacheco roomed with us for a while. Joe Pacheco was a numbers runner and he would often use the dining room table to spread out his pocketful of slips and tabulate his receipts. He really didn't have a room, but slept on a cot in the dining room. People weren't too fussy in those days and were content if someone took them in for cheap, especially if they were single.

Just about everybody played the numbers, even though it was supposed to be a sin. Momma, who was religious up to a point (even though she didn't attend church regularly at the time), could never be shown that there was anything at all wrong with playing the numbers. That was just about the only way that poor people could come by any kind of windfall in those days. You could play the number for a penny on up. Some people even played for a dollar, even two. The highest I ever heard of was when a man hit the number for ten dollars. You played the numbers by picking three digits, using any combination from 000 to 999, which gave you one chance in a thousand of winning. But the payoff was a lot less than that; for each penny you got $5.40 because the numbers banker and his people took the rest. You could play your number "in combination" so that any way the three figures came up together you could win. Of course this cost six times as much as just playing it one way. The runner was paid a small weekly wage and winners were expected to tip the runner ten percent.

Needless to say, a ton of dream books and pamphlets on how to beat the system were sold all over the neighborhood. These books usually associated numbers with the type of dream you had. If you dreamt of walking in the rain, it was one number: if you dreamt of death, it was another. If someone in the family died, everyone played the address. This was also true of marriages, births, accidents, killings, graduations, and whatever else caught the players' fancy. Lacking the mobility, affluence, and economic resources of the average citizen, the numbers provided an important medium of "involvement" for the average black during the depression years and until state lotteries became widespread. Every time a person played, he or she bought the hope of a quick windfall that would come at a time when it was most needed (which was always).

(Players didn't rely on the runners to tell them what number was the winner each day; the game was usually based on three digits in the payoff of a horse in a particular race at a local track. It would appear in the papers and everybody knew what it was every day.)

In the West Indian community, a common practice was to organize clubs for the purpose of saving money. About 12 people would band together and pool a fixed amount of money each week, say, for example, five dollars each. At that rate every week, one person would receive the whole "Pot" or sixty dollars. There were many variations in the amounts put up in these various groups—but the formula was basically the same. The members of such a group were called partners and they were said to be "throwing partners." At times in some of the expanded groups, the treasurer would sometimes disappear with the money amid a good deal of anguish, pathos, and scandal on the community's grapevine. Soon West Indian lodges and civic organizations began to establish informal banks where one could take out a loan, especially for the purpose of mortgages and home improvements. After some years, this practice developed into more substantial businesses called credit unions, which still exist in the West Indian communities in Brooklyn. The importance of these lodge credit unions was that they made funds available, however limited, to many members who would routinely be turned away at the bank.

Nonetheless, to most, the numbers game was the thing. The fact that the chances of winning were 1000 to 1 seemed irrelevant to people who most often found the odds against them to be 1000 to none. Of course, there were 999 losers, for every winner, but once in a while, several people would be winners, and the "banks" would sometimes have difficulty paying off. Other times the runner would "forget" to put in a number (pocketing the bet himself).

The bank was the station that the number runners sent the numbers to. This was usually a sub-station that reported to still a higher source. Playing the numbers was illegal, and the police could pick up runners. There were, in fact, raids from time to time. But usually the police were paid off and cooperated. The numbers game was by far the biggest source of graft the black community paid to the police, lawyers, judges, and people high up in municipal government.

Numbers bankers were usually known as prominent sources of philanthropy in the black community. One young West Indian banker in Harlem, for example, was directly responsible for scores of West Indian

young women being trained in the US as registered nurses. Numbers
bankers were called on to start, support, or save many black businesses
that could not get a dime from local banks. They gave liberally to
churches and many were highly respected in the black community.

The great success of the numbers game in the black community
paved the way for its downfall, because the Mafia moved in. Now these
blacks were used to a little territorial squabble or two, but they were
no match for the methodical, deadly, shootout tactics of the Mafia
(these blacks were certainly not ready to die). The Mafia was a deadly
organization, and in no time at all, they had the bankers in the black
community working for and taking orders from them.

Dutch Schultz, the flamboyant underworld character of the 1930s
and 1940s was a case in point. Joe Pacheco, our roomer, was operating
at the street level in the numbers operation along with many others in
any black neighborhood.

One thing I remember about Joe Pacheco was that he had a car. It
wasn't a flashy car at all—probably third or fourth hand—but it was a
big deal in our neighborhood in 1935. It was the first time in my life
that I had ever ridden in a private car. I was 11 at the time. Once in
a while, Joe would give us kids a ride around a block or two. One day
he took a bunch of us kids to the city (Harlem in Manhattan). We went
over the Brooklyn Bridge, through Manhattan and up to Harlem. We
must have been in the famous Sugar Hill section of Harlem, because
the steepness of the streets in that section reminded us of the roller
coaster at Coney Island. We were all very excited and felt that we had
gone to another world. And by car!

Opportunities to ride in a private car were very few throughout my
growing up. In fact, that ride to Harlem, and a couple of turns around
the neighborhood, represented my total involvement with private cars
through my adolescence. I only remember knowing two other people
who owned cars—the father of Herby Cave, who was an independent
contractor, and the father of Maurice Greaves, who was a Post Office

clerk. I was 12 at the time. In fact, I remember my brother saying that his life ambition at the time was to be a Post Office clerk, because Mr. Greaves owned his own three-family home and had a car on St. Andrews Place, which was headquarters for our group—where we played handball, punchball, stickball, stoopball, touch football, and downs (blocking football).

Maurice's father, Mr. Greaves, hated us to play touch football on the block when his car was parked there in front of his house. This particular day, he forbade us to play because his car was out there. Well, we continued to play, and he stood by watching us—getting madder by the minute. Finally, a long pass was overthrown and hit his car and Mr. Greaves was hot after this crazily bouncing football. He was quite a tall man, about six feet two, and looked awkward chasing the crazily bouncing ball. We were all either too afraid or respectful to try to retrieve the ball, so everyone sort of froze, watching Mr. Greaves.

Just as the ball was about to stop, Mr. Greaves caught up with it, but he slightly overran the ball, and stepped on it. His feet flew out from under him and pointed to the sky. He landed high up on his backside. Our first impulse was to run. Mr. Greaves struggled to regain his feet, holding his backside, the part he landed on. We rounded the corner with a full head of steam and actually rolled on the ground laughing. Mr. Greaves, looking sheepish, held out the ball and offered it back to us. We hesitated, but came forward and accepted it. Mr. Greaves retreated into the house and never again said anything to us about playing football where he parked his car.

When we lived at 1448 Fulton Street, my first cousin, Sybil, came to room with us for a while. Many of the West Indians who moved to America brought much of their way-of-life with them. West Indian parents were generally extremely strict with their children, sometimes to an almost fanatical degree. The West Indian parent considered the American way of life too loose compared to West Indian standards. Children, for the most part, were to be seen rather than heard. Children's

temper tantrums or fits of rage were practically unheard of in a West
Indian home. There was little permissiveness shown by the average
mother or father. Kids kept out of trouble, not for fear of the police but
for fear of their parents. Although my mother was generally strict and
had a no-nonsense attitude about duties, she was more lenient than
most West Indians. This was in part probably due to the fact that my
father was an American.

In many ways, West Indian parents possessed a great deal of love
and compassion for their children, but this seldom took the place of
discipline and obedience. They firmly believed that to spare the rod
was to spoil the child. If his teacher slapped the average West Indian
child, he never reported it to his parents, because he knew full well
that he would be in for another slap or thrashing at home. When I was
at P.S. 93 there was one parent in particular who really put on a show
when she had to go to the school because of her son's misbehavior.
She would chase him around the classroom and, upon catching him,
give him a sound thrashing right in front of the class, to the delight of
his classmates. There were some similar incidents among American
blacks, but by and large, they seemed more permissive with their
children.

Sybil and Ira, my mother's sister's children, and my first cousins,
had been born in Panama. During the building of the Panama Canal,
West Indians descended on Panama from all over the Caribbean
seeking employment on the canal project. My Aunt Meta and her
husband, Allen Yearwood, were among them. They left Barbados for
Panama, so Ira and Sybil were born there. Aunt Meta came to the US
a few years after my mother left Barbados. When Ira and Sybil came
here, we were living at 485 St. Marks Avenue and I was just starting
school. I was about five years old and Ira and Sybil were about nine
and twelve. They helped me with my reading and writing. Aunt Meta
was a grouchy woman who worked hard as a day house-worker and
saved every penny she could to try to get her two boys here after her two

daughters arrived. Their father, Allen Yearwood, was always addressed by my aunt by his surname. We all called him Uncle Yearwood. The thing we remember about him most was that he was an extremely black man and generally had nothing to say to us.

Ira spent more time with us because she was closer to our age. We considered her a big sister and my sister called on her whenever anyone would try to bother us.

Sybil grew into a dark, willowy beauty, and at the age of 17 or 18 when she came to room with us, she was quite a stunning young lady. To add to it, she had a pronounced dimple in her cheek and a mole on her chin, which was the rage in those days. Many West Indian children reached a crisis with their parents at around Sybil's age, as they attempted to participate in the society around them. West Indian parents, particularly "Bajans" (Barbadians), believe that you are a child until you leave home—no matter the age. When you come home after the prescribed hour, or go and come as you please, without explanation, or resist queries by them, they assume you were ready to "make it alone." Many a battle has been waged in the West Indian community among growing son and daughter and father and mother over the rights of parent and child.

So it was with Sybil and her father. That's why Sybil asked my mother if she could stay with us until she got her life straightened out. I was glad that Sybil moved in with us. Even though our space was cramped, she had a tiny room for herself. I was just at the age of puberty and becoming increasingly aware of the other sex. So the coming of a beautiful grown-up cousin was a more than welcome addition to the household. Sybil stayed with us just a few months, till she earned enough money to get a little apartment and fix it up for herself. I remember because it had one of the first refrigerators I'd ever seen.

At the time, Sybil, who had graduated from Girls High School, was working in a rhinestone jewelry factory. She was doing piecework, and she brought much of it home. Many an evening my sister and I sat with her with toothpick and glue, setting rhinestones into brooches and pins. Sybil taught us how to apply the rhinestones and soon we were fairly good at it. We spent many evenings setting rhinestones and chatting.

Although most poor New Yorkers stayed in their neighborhoods, the Daily News and the black press would bring the condition of blacks vividly to their doors. Lynchings were still fairly common in the South and such cases as the Scottsboro Boys were sensationalized. As I became older, I began to think about being born black in America. I would sometimes sit and ponder the question of black and white.

It occurred to me one day that the Civil War didn't come a bit too soon. If it had come, say, twenty-five or thirty years later, we might have been in much more of a dilemma than we were. I began to think this because I noticed that my cousins Vivian and Willie Mae were much lighter in complexion than I was. I also noticed that my father, mother, and I were just about the same color. My first cousins on my mother's side, Sybil and Ira, were darker than we were.

After doing a little investigating, I found out that as generation after generation of slaves evolved, many of them were getting lighter in color. This was due to what was called miscegenation, or the mating of slave owners and overseers with their female slaves. After about a hundred or so years of this, the situation could become quite critical—depending on the philosophy of the plantation you were living on.

One day I looked up the word "miscegenation" in the dictionary and began to muse—suppose a female slave becomes pregnant from her master or overseer—her child was called a half-breed or mulatto. Seventeen years later, this mulatto child became pregnant from her master—this offspring was called a quadroon. Still a slave, but three-quarters white. Now, this child grows up and has a child from her master, things began to get really complicated. In some households it was becoming increasingly difficult to tell slaves from their masters. After mulatto, quadroon, and octoroon, the next offspring was usually so white that they couldn't even find a label to give such a child. Often they moved to another state or city and blended into the white world; they "passed."

Complexions got so light and tangled up that one unwitting plantation master sent his son born of his wife out in the cotton fields every day for a month and allowed his son of his slave mistress to loll around the house until an observant overseer finally brought it to his attention. This often-told story had many variations and became the basis for Mark Twain's novel *Puddin'head Wilson*.

After emancipation, many of these favored offspring were sent to the newly formed schools for former slaves and American Indians such as Tuskegee and Hampton Institute and Howard University. In many ways, this solved a problem that, in another 30 years without the Civil War, would probably have gotten completely out of hand. Right after the Civil War, swarms of schoolteachers were sent from the North by various abolitionist missionary societies to begin the job of educating the Negro masses. Naturally, the first chosen were the Negroes who were further ahead in reading, writing, and general manners. Of course, they were predominantly the man-servants, cooks, butlers, yard boys and nurse maids, the so-called "house Negroes," who were almost invariably, to some degree, related to their masters and therefore were usually of skin color ranging from medium brown to so-called white. This preference by the missionary societies, whatever their intentions, created a visible schism in the black society that placed light skinned blacks ahead of their darker skinned brothers and sisters, a condition that continued until the civil rights movement of the 1960s.

Frederick Douglass, Booker T. Washington and the great majority of blacks who succeeded in business, in the ministry, and in the leadership of the black community were of mixed blood. The Negroes who were trained by the missionaries became the teachers in the grammar schools and high schools all over the black South. They also became the merchants, politicians, caterers, and leaders of black social organizations. It must also be noted that most teachers in the South and in much of the North (black and white) hardly ever had more than what is called a "normal" school education, roughly two years of schooling after high school. However, this was more than adequate to teach the large numbers of blacks, old and young, who flocked to the schoolhouses.

During the mid-1930s, at the height of the depression, my father lost his job at the Aaron Levy slaughterhouse. So, like millions of others, he went to work for the W.P.A. (Works Progress Administration), which was a government agency to keep people working. The W.P.A. created federal jobs for the unemployed. Whether they were artists or ditch-diggers, painters, mechanics, musicians, day laborers, apprentices, craftsmen, all received the same pay. A song came out during the time called "W.P.A.," which made fun of the supposed slow pace of these workers. After protests, it was banned from the radio, but there was many a chuckle about that song, and accusing someone's momma or poppa of being on the W.P.A. became a familiar part of the "dozens," a street game we played.

We were also allowed to go to the local relief station to get fresh vegetables and other food staples that were being given away by the government. The station was located only a half block away from where we lived at 1448 Fulton Street, but I wished it were at least a mile from home. There was always a long line outside, and I hated being seen on that line. I was only about 11 or 12 years old, but I didn't want to have any part of any giveaway. I would pull my cap down over my eyes and keep my head facing the other way until my turn came. My mother hated to send me, but she had no choice at the time. She also hated accepting charity. As soon as we were able, she didn't let me go anymore.

The most notable racial disturbance during my youth was one that we read about that took place in Harlem in the mid 1930s. Along

125<sup>th</sup> Street, which was the main thoroughfare, a teenager was caught stealing in a busy 5&10-cent store. After a struggle he was subdued by workers in the store and then taken downstairs into the basement. One of the blacks in the store at the time ran to the street and reported that the boy had been beaten. There had been several incidents of friction between the police and Harlem blacks preceding this one, and word spread quickly. Before long, an angry mob had gathered a few blocks away. One thing led to another and soon, store windows were broken and innocent people beaten. Meanwhile, the police had spirited the boy out of the store basement to police headquarters. When the mob reached the store and the boy could not be produced, they became more incensed and rampaged down the street, destroying property along the way. One of the amusing stories passed around was that the mob came down a street in Harlem, breaking store windows and looting, as they approached a Chinese restaurant. The owner, thinking only of trying to save his business, rushed out into the street shouting, "Me nigga too! Me nigga too!," totally unaware that word was a derogatory remark in the black community when uttered by anyone other than a black person.

A notable phenomenon of the 1930s was the almost total absence of black teachers in the elementary schools of New York City, despite a large black population. This was due in part to the fact that the initial migration of blacks to New York from the South occurred during World War I to work in war production jobs. There was a shortage of labor because of the much-increased production to supply the Allies and the drafting of young men. Blacks were offered the bottom jobs in industry, but these were jobs they could not get before the war.

In the South, the most respected job in the black community (besides the few doctors and lawyers) was that of a schoolteacher. There was plenty of opportunity to teach in the South at a low salary, and the black teacher was secure in her environment. I say "her" because black teachers in the public schools were overwhelmingly female. In the cities of the South, elementary teachers, black and white, were highly respected. Most of the teachers who graduated with degrees from the black colleges like Hampton, Fisk, Howard and Morgan, taught in the black high schools and normal schools. During the 1930s and early 1940s, most of the black teachers in the South were living middle-class lives and taking care of the black children of the South and had no thought of moving to the uncertainties of the North. The standard of "separate but equal" supported by the efforts of Booker T. Washington had sadly broken down and the black schools were far below the standards of white schools.

In New York City, a highly sophisticated environment as far as education was concerned, blacks and West Indians were a distinct minority in most of the districts where blacks lived. Also, there was no separate but equal standard, which created the large employment of black teachers in the South. In New York City, it was necessary to have a bachelor's degree, and to be able to pass the State Regents examination before getting a teaching job. Some black teachers from the South and the West Indies could have met these standards, and beyond, but by and large, they had no desire to leave the comforts of teaching in their home environment. Just like the great emigration from Europe in the late 1800s, it was primarily the poor who were driven to distant shores.

Consequently, in the three elementary schools I attended—P.S. 42, first and third grade; P.S. 83, fourth grade; and P.S. 93, fifth grade to eighth grade—and all the way through four years at Brooklyn Automotive High School, I was taught by only one black teacher in the fourth grade, a Mrs. Pearson, who was a veteran teacher in the New York City school system.

Most of the teachers I had were fair in their treatment of us. I was somewhat of a discipline problem. From the fifth grade through the seventh, my mother had to be summoned to the school because of minor infractions. During my eighth grade, I had no such problem;

Miss Ellis, an elderly, grouchy woman tolerated no foolishness in her class. The next semester, I had Miss Nelson, who had even the "baddest" children purring like kittens. There was never so much as a sound in her class. Even coughing was held to a minimum. She was a blondish woman with large breasts that stood out in front of her and a large rear that stood out behind her. Reflecting on this, years later, she reminded me of the classic Wagnerian diva. I always wondered how she controlled a class far better than anyone else, taught more than anyone else, and was regarded by her students, mostly in retrospect, as the best teacher they ever had.

Mrs. Rudder, my 7A teacher, was a young brunette whom I had a real crush on, but she seemed disappointed in me, as I didn't finish the term with anything near the potential I had started with. Mrs. Moiyo, a typical Italian mother-type, taught me in 7B, and I got my only real slap from a teacher, which was well deserved, from her. She had a sister, a Mrs. Caleo, who also taught me in 5B. My 6B teacher was Miss Diffenderfer. She and her sister, both spinsters, and German, wore old-fashioned clothing and high shoes that laced halfway up the calf.

Miss Diffenderfer was a good teacher and controlled her class well. The memorable thing about her was that she started each day by reading a chapter from the Bible. Her favorite was the 23rd Psalm and I almost remember it by heart. Her voice was very sincere and serene as she read:

> Yea, though I walk through the valley of the shadow of death,
> I will fear no evil: For thou art with me;
> Thy rod and thy staff, they comfort me . . .
> Surely goodness and mercy shall follow me all the days of my life, and I will dwell in the House of the Lord forever.

There were three or four male teachers but I never had one as an official teacher. I had a Mr. McMahon for science in the seventh grade, but he was completely neurotic, had no control over his class whatsoever, and taught very little. Mr. Simon, a likeable young man, was my gym teacher in the eighth grade.

During the 1930s, a much broader range of nationalities were represented in the school system including Italian, Irish, German, and American. The number of Jewish teachers who stayed out on Jewish holidays was hardly enough to disrupt the system. The Jewish predominance in the teaching ranks seemed to start during the 1940s.

Brooklyn children considered themselves especially fortunate to have the first Thursday in June off. Psychologically, we felt even better, knowing that the kids in the other boroughs had to go to school. This day was called Anniversary Day in honor of the schools in the Brooklyn Sunday School Union. All of the Sunday schools in Brooklyn had parades in their neighborhoods with Sunday school and church flags leading their sections. The boy and girl scout troops paraded and all the various classes were assembled. It was a big day for us kids. Everyone got dressed up for the parade and a scout troop drum and bugle corps led each church group. I played bugle in the St. Phillips Boy Scout Drum and Bugle Corps. There was much rivalry among the drum corps. Often the marchers were restricted to one side of the street because another group was coming down the other. As the corps passed each other, they played their loudest, attempting to drown out the other troop or make them lose their step.

It was a colorful parade and everyone had on their Sunday best. After the parade that afternoon, the marchers assembled back at their respective churches for a picnic lunch, sodas, and ice cream.

Back in those days, hot water was a commodity fairly hard to come by, because we always lived in "cold water" flats. That meant that to get hot water, you lit a cylindrical gas burner in the kitchen that had a copper coil running through it to heat enough water for you to fill the tub. This heated water was treated as a precious commodity because the gas bill was to be kept as low as possible. Saturday night was the general bath night, so that you would be all ready for Sunday school the next morning. Bathing during the week was restricted to "sponge offs," except for special occasions.

Although my father had little to say at home, he would never allow ironing while the radio was playing, as this, to him, was too much of a drain on the electric current.

The radio was the means of information as well as entertainment during the 1930s, and many of the most revered names in American entertainment were starting out at the time. This was also the heyday of the radio serials—The Lone Ranger, Little Orphan Annie, and Jack Armstrong were the leading serials. The comic shows were Jack Benny, Fanny Brice, Fred Allen, and Joe Penner, with Edgar Bergen and Charlie McCarthy coming a bit later. There was a horror show called *The Inner Sanctum* that we kids used to go to each other's houses and sit around the living room with the lights out to fully enjoy.

*Buck Rogers in the 25th Century* was our view of the future, and the A-bomb was nowhere in sight. We heard a bit about Albert Einstein and the theory of relativity but knew nothing about it. Who did?

Although I took it pretty much for granted at the time, it was years later that I realized that I had come along during the heyday of Tin Pan Alley, when nearly all the great standard songs we still hear were written. I knew the words and music to most of the songs of George and Ira Gershwin, Cole Porter, Hoagy Carmichael, Irving Berlin and Jerome Kern, and the songs from the big movie musicals starring Fred Astaire and Ginger Rogers, Dick Powell, Alice Faye, Nelson Eddy and Jeanette MacDonald. The jazz and blues of such greats like Lil Green ("In the Dark"), Billie Holiday ("Strange Fruit"), Louis Armstrong ("I'll Be Glad When You're Dead, You Rascal You"), Jimmy Lunceford ("For Dancers Only"), Duke Ellington ("In a Sentimental Mood"), Coleman

Hawkins ("Body and Soul"), Erskine Hawkins ("Tuxedo Junction"), and the Swing era of the big white bands such as Tommy Dorsey ("Marie"), Glen Miller ("String of Pearls"), Charlie Barnett ("Cherokee"), Artie Shaw ("Begin the Beguine"), and many more—all this music I knew by heart, practically note for note, riff for riff. But in those days, this was not uncommon.

The New York World's Fair of 1939-1940 was an exciting time, with people converging on New York from around the world. We went with our class at school at least twice, besides making a couple of trips with family. Relatives came up from the South on a couple of occasions to see the fair and stayed at our apartment.

There were always long lines that required at least a two-hour wait to see the most popular exhibit which was put on by Consolidated Edison, our local electric company. But when your turn came and you sat down in that car that carried you through the exhibit, it was a thrilling sequence. It started with a voice saying "Night falls on the city of light" and in front of you was a miniature New York City and the car took you to all its major points. I saw it twice. Billy Rose's Aquacade featuring Eleanor Holmes was another popular feature of the fair. The posters that advertised Sally Rand, the controversial fan dancer, also intrigued us.

I grew up under the colorful mayor Fiorello H. LaGuardia, a short round robust Italian-Portuguese-Jewish politician who read comics to us over the radio on Sundays during a newspaper strike and was well liked by the people of New York City.

One of the positive things about going to school in New York City was the class trips you went on to such places as the Hayden Planetarium, the Museum of Natural History, the Metropolitan Museum of Art, the Brooklyn Botanic Gardens and the Bronx Zoo.

Years later while studying music and during my introduction to classical music, I remembered the music appreciation classes that I had in grammar school at PS 93. The music teacher taught us words that identified a particular melody, such as "March, March, March Slav, 'March Slav' by Tchaikovsky," including the title "March Slav"; and to the slow movement of Schubert's *Unfinished Symphony*, "This is the symphony that Schubert wrote but never finished"; "Morning is coming and birds are humming, / 'Morning' from *Peer Gynt* by Grieg"; "My Elegie, My Elegie, Massenet," for "Elegie" by Massenet; "Humoresque, The world is blest, And you have brought a happy thought to every heartsick mortal here below," for "Humoresque" by Dvorak. A plaintive and lovely melody that always reminds me of this period when I hear it is Edward McDowell's "To a Wild Rose" from *Woodland Sketches*. For some reason that plaintive melody has been a consolation to me all my life.

There was a street word game that we played called "the dozens." A favorite retort to someone who called you a name you didn't like would be "your mother." If he said you were ugly, you said, "your mother." If he called you a bastard, you said, "your mother." Then it proceeded to a contest of one-upmanship as to who could win these word games with the cleverest retorts, which included rhymed verse and the most vulgarly graphic descriptions that you could muster. This exercise could end in a few words, or continue at length, depending upon the will, or skill if you will, of the participants. This was always carried on with a few onlookers either signifying or responding to the situation with guffaws and ad-lib commentary.

The "dozens" was a pretty rough game but you had to try to be good-humored about it growing up in our neighborhoods. Almost all kids in the poor areas played the "dozens," so if you didn't, your only alternative was to fight, and you'd be fighting all the time. As crude as it was, it tested the imagination and ingenuity of many a youngster in creating the original rhymes and clichés that got the laughs. It is probable that many a songwriter and rapper got his introduction to poetry through playing the "dozens." A couple of the retorts would go like this: "You call me sun because I shine, but I call you son because you're mine." "I fucked your momma and your sister too, I went to fuck your father but the bastard flew." And so it went.

The use of words, phrases, metaphors, poems, lies, and deceit is all combined to put your rival "down" with as much humor and outrageous commentary involving his mother's habits, loves, sex life, and especially your particular access to her sexually. Since it was more like an amusing verbal sport, there were seldom any hard feelings afterwards. Originally, this term was used at a point in argument when all respect for your adversary ceased—somewhat like a slap in the face with a glove, the next order of business being to establish the time and place of a duel by sword or pistol in an earlier era.

Among the black kids of New York, this word—motherfucker—had been refined to the point of merely expressing mild anger, sarcasm, surprise, joy, even an affectionate greeting or a variety of other sentiments depending on the tone, inflection, or volume of delivery. (A good contemporary example of this is demonstrated by Richard Pryor in the 1982 film *Live on the Sunset Strip*.) It is also much used as a reference to a third person or persons.

Almost all kids used the term, but among many of the "street cats" or guys who hung around the local poolrooms, street corners, and the like, motherfucker became a word that took up more and more of the vocabulary until there was scarcely room for anything else. It came to mean almost everything and everybody. It was the all-around uptown pronoun. When greeting a friend it was "Hi, motherfucker." If a pair of shoes was seen in the window, the words to describe them were: "Man, look at them mfs. They about some bad motherfuckers, ain't they?" When referring to a third person, "I saw that motherfucker yesterday, and he was as mad as a motherfucker." If suddenly angered, "Fuck you, motherfucker! Mess with me, motherfucker, and I'll kick your motherfuckin' ass." It had gotten to the point where one "cat" would call another a "motherfuckin' motherfucker."

As a young kid growing up, I had about three definite ways of expressing myself. One was at home with no curse words (the word "damn" was considered a curse word in our house), one in the street with some curse words, and one around the guys where you could really let go. Of course, there were several refinements and gradations in between, depending on the occasion or circumstance. It was automatic. You never had to think twice. You just spoke, and the right words came out to fit the situation.

My father swore like a sailor when he was drunk, which was every weekend, but nobody else did. Momma was capable of a couple of cuss words when we overly provoked her, and her favorite expression was "You all is a pain, . . . *in* the ass."

The first and last birthday party I had growing up was on July 29th, my eleventh birthday, while we were living in that hellhole at 1342 Fulton Street. Most of the people who came were adult relatives from my father's side of the family and the favorite drink was homemade "bathtub" gin. It was also the day I found out that my real birthday was on July 28th, not the 29th.

Aunt Melissa had come up from Washington, and there was lots of loud talking and guffawing. An old friend of Momma's was there, and she pointed out that her daughter was born on the same day as I was, the 28th. Momma remembered this and checked it out later, to find that the woman was right. My sister was born a year earlier than I in Cumberland Street Hospital, but my brother and I were both delivered by midwives at home—at the time, still a common practice among the poor. Momma probably confused the date when she later recorded my birth at the Board of Health, but from then on, I celebrated on the 28th.

But the most memorable events of the evening had to do with smells I'll never forget. First our dog, Spike, took a large crap right in the middle of the living room rug, which embarrassed us all. I guess nobody remembered to take him for his walk.

After the party thinned out a bit, my uncle, having had a lot of gin, kicked off his shoes and stretched out on a sofa. A few of the others were still exchanging stories and talking about Colonel Julian, the Black Eagle of Harlem, who had recently challenged the Italians to an air duel. Soon a strange sickening odor began to permeate the room. People started looking around, and they finally settled on my uncle's feet. His feet really smelled bad.

One of the people who came up from Washington had a particular air about himself, and during the evening he had been throwing around a couple of long words that nobody understood. He said that my uncle had a case of halitosis of the feet. This brought a loud guffaw from all of us. That was because there was an ad for Listerine about that time that described halitosis as the scientific word for bad breath, which was of course cured by the mouthwash. The same man also observed that between Spike and my uncle, the evening began and ended on a smelly note. Another guest, who was the self-styled comic of the evening, threw a nearby clothes bag over my uncle's feet and exclaimed, "Man, we should have sent this one to Ethiopia to fight them Italians. All they would have to do would be to put him in the front lines and tell him to take his shoes off—and the war would be over."

I don't know whether the events of the day had anything to do with it, but actually, that was my last birthday party. The fact is that I was 11 years old, but I can hardly remember any children being at the party. It was mostly for relatives on my father's side of the family. After that, on my birthday, Momma just baked a cake and we ate it for dessert after dinner.

Spike was also the first and last dog we ever had. He resembled a medium-sized hunting dog with heavy skin that you could grab and pull up from his backbone. We really thought we were "putting it on" to have a dog, and Spike liked to run up and down the streets and around the block with us.

One day at dinner, Spike was in his familiar sitting position—looking up at us with sad eyes as though we were eating his food. The porcelain tabletop in the kitchen was a bit uneven and so were the plate bottoms. We found that this caused a plate to rotate or turn slightly on the table when you pushed it on the edge with your hand. We thought we had really discovered something. This particular night we had spaghetti and meatballs. Evelyn and Will and I would call out: "Spaghetti" or "Meatball" and push the plate. It would make a half turn or so. We would try to guess if it would stop at what we called. Naturally, the harder we spun the plate, the more times it would go around. We got it up to one and a half to two times spinning before the plate would stop. I was determined to beat this, so I hollered "Meatball!" and gave the plate its hardest spin. At this speed, the meatball flew off the plate and off the table. Spike, sitting there in his usual position, caught it on the fly before you could blink an eye. I grabbed Spike by the throat and wrestled him to the floor, but he had caught and swallowed the meatball in the same motion. When I let Spike go, he scrambled to his feet, a bewildered and hurt expression on his face, and slowly retreated into another room. My sister and brother were cracking up with laughter, and I had spaghetti minus meatball for dinner.

My father had brought Spike home one day and told us a friend of his had given him the dog as a present. Momma never took to the dog. She claimed we had nothing that anybody would want to steal so we didn't need a watchdog. And having another mouth to feed—even dog food—was beyond the family budget.

Once Momma walked the dog about eight blocks from home and then hid from him, hoping to lose him. But when she got home, Spike was already there. Another time she got Joe Pacheco, our roomer, to drive her a couple miles from home with the dog, but in about two hours, Spike was back.

Daddy particularly liked Spike because whenever he spoke, even gently, Spike would start to tremble, turn in circles and wag his tail ferociously, and then approach my father with his head held low. I believe this gave Daddy a feeling of power, which he relished, but could not summon up from the rest of the family. So he called Spike as often as he could. Spike was the first name we usually heard him call out as he reached our floor coming home from work.

One day, after Spike had been with us six or seven months and was full-grown, he didn't show up in the evening after running around the neighborhood. We kids looked up and down the street for him till, about two days later, Spike turned the corner toward our house. He looked awful, and we were frightened. Spike was very dirty, mangy-looking, with his fur matted up in spots. He hardly looked like the Spike we knew at all. Not knowing what to do, we sneaked him into the house and gave him a bath in the tub. Then we fed him. He came around nicely.

A couple of weeks later, Spike disappeared again and was gone another couple of days. When he returned, he looked even worse than before—and he was dragging. Momma saw him first and refused to let him into the house. We got some food to him, and when Momma left for work the next day, we cleaned him up again.

The third time happened about two weeks later, and this time Spike didn't make it back. We sort of looked for him, but he never turned that corner again. He was our first and last dog.

My mother "broke" me at an early age from being left-handed—at least around the house. Being left-handed in those days was a bit more difficult than today because most things were built for right-handed people. I also believe that Momma, being rather superstitious, considered it an unwelcome omen—like some kind of influence of the devil.

I was not allowed to eat with my left hand. I was trained to do most things at home with my right hand. I wrote with my right hand. I drew with my right hand. But I punched, batted, swung, hit, and had my greatest strength in my left hand. I called my right hand my skill hand and my left hand my brute hand. At the time it seemed a small war was waging about the psychological effects of making a child right-handed who was naturally left-handed. But my mother never had any doubt about her convictions.

As growing kids, we all had our baseball heroes and sometimes, through the Boy Scouts and the Knot Hole Gang (a charity for children), we got to see a ball game at Ebbets Field—the home of the Brooklyn Dodgers. We collected bubble gum cards and rooted for the Dodgers, Giants or Yankees like most any other kids. Cookie Lavagetto, Pee Wee Reese, Duke Snider, and Dolph Camilli were the "Boys of Summer" to us—even though none of these players were black. We never thought about this very much. It was like—this is the way it's supposed to be. There were no black baseball players in the big leagues, no black football players, no black basketball players, no black tennis players, and no black jockeys.

Years later, I found out that at the turn of the century, most jockeys who rode the Derby and all the other famous races were black. This stopped when the jockeys began to be represented by agents and the jockeys were cut in for ten percent of the winning stake. Many of the exercise boys and grooms remained black, but all the black jockeys disappeared. In professional sports, only in boxing could a black man compete against a white man, and blacks soon dominated the sport with such standouts as Jack Johnson, Kid Chocolate, Henry Armstrong, Joe Louis, Ray Robinson, and Joe Walcott.

During the fights of Joe Louis in particular, the black community took on an almost carnival atmosphere with radios blaring, people huddling in groups and bars full of eager, boisterous patrons listening to the fight over the radio. When Joe Louis put one of his foes away with a knockout punch, the porters, delivery boys, dishwashers, ditch diggers, waiters, maids, and jackhammer operators were smiling when they reported to work the next morning.

In amateur sports, blacks excelled in track (you only needed sneakers and shorts and the outdoors). The most renowned of these was the sprinter Jesse Owens, who won four gold medals at the 1936

Olympics held in Germany. Hitler was reported to have snubbed Jesse
Owens as he stood on the winners' pedestal—presumably because he
was black. A lot of Americans, whites as well as blacks, were outraged.
Even though Hitler is regarded by many as one of the most outspoken
racists of all time, I have reexamined this incident in retrospect.

The year 1936 was a time when racial prejudice was virulent both in
Germany (primarily against the Jews) and in the U.S.A. (primarily against
the blacks). Hitler scorned the United States for winning with what he
called "the United States and its African legions"—hence, his snub of
Owens. Could it be that Hitler's attitude was that the "civilized" countries
of the world were involved in a gentlemanly contest among amateur
athletes, and only citizens in good standing could be characterized as
gentlemen? This "African legion" that he referred to were the American
"citizens" who could not mix in most of the organized sports in the US
itself—who, in many states in 1936, could not drink at white public
fountains, could not belong to white clubs, were relegated to the back
of buses and trains, could not use many public parks or swimming pools
or drink a Coke or eat a hamburger at a drugstore lunch counter in the
capital of the United States, who were still being lynched frequently—yet,
complains Hitler, you send these second-class citizens to mingle with
the gentlemen of the world. Could it be that what Hitler was saying was
that he practiced discrimination in Germany, yes, but there were no
Jews on his team? Could Hitler have been saying "Why should I give
first-class respect to an American black when he can't get it from his
own nation?" But the American press looked upon this incident only as
proof of Hitler's racism, which was characterized by Hitler's relentless
campaign against the Jews that culminated in the gas chambers of World
War II. The alternative consideration of elevating the American black
to first-class status in 1936 never entered anyone's mind.

During the mid-1930s, Italy ruled a piece of Africa they called
Italian Somalia. It bordered on Ethiopia, the only continuously

independent black nation in Africa. All of the other black nations in Africa were dominated by foreign powers. The Italian fascist leader Benito Mussolini had joined Hitler in his campaign of conquest and terror prior to World War II and moved on Ethiopia in 1935. The newspapers and radios carried daily reports of the Italian invasion. The Ethiopians had swords, spears, sticks and some mounted cavalry with antiquated rifles to face the invaders. The Italians had modern arms, tanks, airplanes, and were reported to be using dum-dum bullets (bullets that explode on impact) against the sadly outgunned defenders.

The Italians penetrated deeper and deeper into Ethiopia. Haile Selassie, the Emperor of Ethiopia, appeared before the League of Nations in Geneva, Switzerland, and appealed to the great powers of the world to intercede against the fascists. What was the League for? Up to that time, no European power had ever come to the aid of an African nation in distress, so nothing was done beyond voicing disapproval of the fascist aggression.

Enlistment centers were set up in New York and other major cities primarily by Marcus Garvey, the self-styled "black liberator" from Jamaica (the man who first said: "Black is Beautiful") and his followers and other black nationalist groups. Thousands of black volunteers across the country were reportedly ready to join forces with the Ethiopians to fight the fascists. But the logistics of this was compounded by the Atlantic Ocean and the rigid enforcement of U. S. neutrality laws. Actually, only two blacks reached Ethiopia, and one of them was the self-styled "Black Eagle," Hubert Fauntleroy Julian.

Julian had come to New York in 1921 from Trinidad, West Indies, and was an officer in Garvey's "African Legion" in the 1920s. He flew an airplane and gained much notoriety by performing daredevil feats and some parachute jumps over Harlem. Amid much publicity, he planned the first solo flight to Africa. He was outfitted with a plane called Ethiopia. Amid much fanfare and an audience of 15,000 people, he took off on July 4, 1924. But a few minutes later the plane crashed-landed in the mud flats of Jamaica Bay. He crawled from the wreckage and vowed to try again.

His exploits had previously won Julian an invitation from the then Ras Tafari Mahonnen to his coronation as Emperor Haile Selassie of Ethiopia, and Julian had sailed for Ethiopia on April 25, 1930. At the coronation, Julian stunted above the field for one hour, and later parachuted from 5,000 feet—the first jump in Ethiopian history. The emperor was highly impressed and made Julian a colonel in the Ethiopian army and commander of the three-plane Ethiopian Air Force—and proclaimed him a national hero. Later, after he had disobeyed an imperial order and wrecked a new government airplane, Selassie banished the flamboyant Julian from Ethiopia.

Unknown to the masses in America, the relationship between Selassie and Julian further deteriorated to the point that, at one time, Julian was said to be in the employ of the Italian government and had changed his name to Huberto Fauntleroyana Juliano. But when the Italians invaded Ethiopia, Julian, from his vantage point in New York performed some air maneuvers and challenged the entire Italian air force to a duel. He was a majestic figure in his helmet, goggles, and scarf, waving from the cockpit of a real plane. The black press gave him ample space and the black community, solidly behind Ethiopia, delighted in the exploits of the brash, colorful, exuberant Colonel Julian. He became something of a folk hero—a sort of real live "Smilin' Jack" or "Mandrake the Magician" of comic strip fame.

The Italians overran Ethiopia, but it was the eve of the Spanish Civil War and then World War II, one outcome of which was that Italy lost all its colonies in Africa, and Haile Selassie returned to rule Ethiopia.

Though the exploits of the Black Eagle were mostly symbolic to blacks in New York, there was a sense of kinship and participation in the struggle against the fascists. When the Ethiopian-Italian war broke out, I was 11. We kids played a game of matching cards by spinning them to the ground; being a great card spinner, I had won hundreds of bubble gum picture cards that depicted various sports heroes and World War I flying aces like Eddie Rickenbacker and the German Baron von Richthofen. Of course, there was no black World War I flying aces, so Colonel Julian, the Black Eagle, was especially welcome. Rat-a-tat-tat.

It wasn't until the 1940s that significant numbers of black children were introduced to black history, especially in the inner-city schools of the North. There was no mention of blacks in any of the history books other than that they were slaves and had been freed by Abraham Lincoln with the Civil War. The exploits of Crispus Attucks, a black man who fell at the Boston massacre on the eve of the American Revolution, or Harriet Tubman, a leader of the Underground Railroad, or Nat Turner who led a slave revolt in Virginia, or Matthew Henson who discovered the North Pole with Admiral Peary, or Joseph Cinque who led the mutiny of the slave ship Amistad. These and other events of history that would elicit pride in black children and engender hope for the future were generally unknown to them until about the time of World War II or later. This was somewhat corrected by the efforts of black organizations such as the NAACP, the Urban League, the black YMCA, some black church groups and black fraternal orders. Because segregated black schools in the South had black principals and teachers, southern students were generally more aware of black history than those in the North. The teaching of black history in inner-city ghetto schools increased after World War II.

Religion played a role in the lives of most Barbadians and English-speaking West Indians. The Church of England, of their so-called mother country, was Anglican or Episcopal. Later, during the 1930s, evangelical churches became popular with West Indians both at home and in New York.

For most blacks, ostracized and discriminated against at every turn, the church was much more than a place to worship. It was the meeting place—the socio-political base that was used as shelter from a hostile and indifferent world. Poor and uneducated blacks used the church as their place of equality, especially the more liberal, less structured Protestant evangelical denominations such as "holy rollers," Church of God in Christ, Pentecostal, Baptist, Methodist, Holiness, Nazarene. Among their chief attractions was the wide range of expressions that was practiced in these smaller churches such as baptism of adults, getting the spirit, speaking in tongues, clapping, jumping, testifying, and rolling, to the sounds of tambourines, drums, pianos, guitars, and other instruments. A great many of them were "store front" churches with small congregations.

More affluent and educated blacks saw the church as a place to exercise their superior status—lacking any other major forum in the society at large. They became the elders and rulers of the church and thus the models for the community, even though many of these same sisters and brothers hated, cheated, lied, fornicated, stole, and were among the prisoners in the local jails. Of course, many aspects of this situation were prevalent in the whites' structure as well, although seldom with the same zeal and fervor.

Among basic institutions such as housing, the work place, the school and the playground, the least integrated of these has always been the church. This seems to operate by mutual consent of black and white alike. The rationale appears to be that blacks have their own problems to deal with (which are mostly white), and whites have their own problems to deal with (which are often black).

Many blacks take the practical approach, consciously or not, reasoning that if they adopt the white man's religion they will be favored or tolerated to a greater extent than non-believers.

Probably, the single aspect that most influences both black and white is that Christianity is a religion that forgives—that tolerates all the sins that a person is capable of committing and then absolves or forgives sins and transgressions simply by a prayer, a confession, a wave of the hand or a word. Thieves, murderers, kidnappers, whoremongers, racists, all can find refuge in the Christian religion. The Christian religion is based on love.

In the last days of slavery, the strong allegiance of blacks to Christianity stemmed from the fact that abolitionists, who were motivated primarily by religious conviction, led the antislavery movement. But some slaves got their introduction to Scripture as the result of efforts of some slave owners to indoctrinate them into the "docility" of Christianity, and to let them know that in the Bible, no less an authority than God decreed that "the last shall be first"; "your reward will be in heaven"; and "turn the other cheek."

In other cases, slave masters allowed their favored illegitimate slave children to be taught to read the Bible and receive other educational advantages.

About four short blocks from us, when we were at 1342 Fulton Street, Father Devine's Brooklyn "heaven" opened one bright spring Sunday in 1934. I was ten years old.

We were witnessing a happy occasion as we stood on the curb outside the "heaven" on the corner of Macon Street and Marcy Avenue. The "heaven" was actually two brownstone houses in which the main floor interiors had been gutted to make one large room. Devine's female followers, who were called "angels," were dressed in white, and the men in black. There was a parade of his followers, and to us, they seemed to be everywhere. They were all shouting, "Peace, it's truly wonderful" and "Father Devine is God."

Bringing up the rear was a motorcade, in the center of which was Father Devine himself. He rode in a long black, shining limousine with the top down. There were bodyguards running or walking alongside just like they do for a president.

Father Devine was a short, black man, a little on the plump side with a winning smile, who moved about with surety and confidence. He continually waved at the curious throngs lined up on the sidewalk. As Father Devine's limousine pulled up to the front of the "heaven," the din grew into a roar as the believers demonstrated. There were nurses present who gave smelling salts to a couple of people who got too carried away in the heat. Father Devine got out amid the tumult, ascended the stairs, and was soon inside the building where from outside we heard a roar of voices cheering his arrival.

Father Devine was an itinerant preacher who started in the South, but his mission really took-off when he opened a church in Sayville, Long Island, about 50 miles east of New York City. The town contained a small black community that mostly worked as field hands on the potato farms of Long Island and as domestic workers. His spirited and boisterous prayer meetings threatened the tranquility of this mostly lily-white community. When some citizens complained, Devine produced a brilliant coup for himself and his followers, when he and some of his disciples were arrested for disturbing the peace and got one-year jail sentences by Judge Lewis J. Smith. A couple of days after imposing sentence, the judge, 55, dropped dead of a heart attack. Father Devine was quoted in the press as exclaiming, "I hated to do it!" With the help of the publicity of this "miracle," Father Devine's legions grew by leaps and bounds.

The black community was alive with talk of Father Devine. Most of the conservative or better-off blacks considered him an outright fake. But the rank and file were impressed. Many said: "What we need is a black God" and "How we gonna get anywhere bowing to a white God—someone who doesn't look like us?"

Father Devine came right on the heels of Marcus Garvey who, besides arousing the black conscience to a degree never before realized in America, was also in a sense "trying to beat the (white) man at his own game." In his great strivings to uplift the black masses, he founded the Universal Negro Improvement Association (UNIA). His major effort was to launch the Black Star Steamship Line that would "show the world" that the black man could carry on in the world of commerce, the equal of anyone, as well as provide commerce and transport for his Back to Africa Movement.

Garvey tried to get around the image of the white Christian God by founding the African Orthodox Church with a black hierarchy of bishops, priests, brothers, and elders and proclaiming that God was black. Although the essence of the Garvey movement survived to flower again (especially in the civil rights movement of the 1960s), the steamship line foundered, and the African Orthodox Church gradually petered out.

Female followers of both Garvey and Devine were recognizable because of the taboo against "straightening" or putting hot combs in the hair to give it a "relaxed" or "white" look. That style was pioneered some years earlier by Madame Walker, who became one of the first black millionaires primarily through the sale of hair products such as grease, pomades, and oils.

Both Garvey and Devine realized that self-worth started with self-worship. Every people on earth had their own god or gods, who looked exactly like them, except the blacks in the western hemisphere who were removed from their native lands as slaves. The African drum, because of its militant and religious connotations, was absolutely forbidden, on pain of death, by slaveholders in North America. It was permitted in the Caribbean and South America where whites were in a distinct minority—mostly overseers and clerks. Most religions south of the Sahara were centered on a hierarchy of gods representing different needs or aspirations.

Father Devine took the direct approach and had himself proclaimed as God, and rather than set his economic goals on existing standards, he moved to become directly relevant to the masses.

Devine opened a "heaven" in most of the major cities of the US, with Philadelphia as headquarters. He established many small businesses, chiefly restaurants selling meals for 15 cents and barbershops that gave a haircut for a dime. These shops were staffed by his followers and became popular with black people in general especially because it was during the depression of the 1930s. In fact, most black Christians thought nothing of going into one of Father Devine's restaurants and raising their hand and exclaiming, "Peace, it's truly wonderful" which was the prerequisite for buying a meal.

Many blacks reasoned that Father Devine could be God as much as anybody and that at least he was in their own image. He was also feeding poor blacks, providing decent accommodations at rock bottom prices and giving haircuts for a dime. Could anybody top that? In a major depression, that kind of approach was bound to achieve some success, and it did.

A fundamental difference between Garvey and Devine was that Garvey expounded the separation of the races in every detail—there were no white people in the UNIA—and the ultimate ideological goal was to return blacks to their original African homelands. Devine, on the other hand, welcomed whites into his movement. (In fact, his main hotel in Philly was a gift from a white follower.) The fact is that he married a white Canadian "angel" at the height of his popularity, and she sat at his side. The movement proclaimed that all people were equal and all were welcome to follow the Father.

When I was about ten and living at 1342 Fulton Street, I noticed crowds gathering in the evening with people sometimes climbing up small ladders or standing on boxes to speak. As I watched, I learned that they were communists and they were trying to force the White Tower hamburger place on Fulton Street and Nostrand Avenue to hire black people as countermen.

Black and white people were carrying signs asking people not to patronize where you can't work. They chanted and talked and cajoled anyone who tried to enter the store. Little by little, people started to stay away until business fell off to a trickle. This was a 95-percent black neighborhood at the time, and Nostrand and Fulton was the busiest black corner in Brooklyn. Most businesses with jobs of this type, unskilled service jobs, used only white employees, even in all-black neighborhoods and before World War II there were lots of poor whites to fill these jobs. All service jobs, including trolley and bus drivers, milkmen, counter men and women, salesmen, deliverymen, waiters, waitresses, and all but a few cooks, employed whites. Blacks worked in restaurants only as dishwashers, busboys, and cleaning men.

After keeping up the pressure for a few weeks, the protesters finally won, and the whole community was proud to see two black countermen working in White Tower flipping hamburgers. The group then moved a few doors up Fulton Street to the Kresge 5 and 10. A counter girl was paid low wages, but still there were no blacks.

By then the movement had gained momentum, and in a couple of weeks we saw the first black girl at the counters of the 5 and 10 in the heart of the black community in Brooklyn.

It must be remembered that in the 1930s the Communist Party was a legal and fast-growing political force, particularly in New York City, and the leadership of the party was openly fighting social injustices and discrimination, while advocating white and black equality. This was heady stuff to many of the downtrodden blacks newly arriving from the tyranny of the South and the rigid class structure of the West Indies in the mid 1930s.

Until the election of 1932 that brought Franklin D. Roosevelt and the New Deal to power, there was very little consideration given to the black vote by either the Democratic or Republican Party. Most blacks of the time voted Republican. This was simply because Abraham Lincoln, some 65 years before, had been a Republican. And the urban Democratic politicians did not regard the vote of the newly settled blacks as of any real significance until the 1940s. Blacks had, till then, very little concentrated voting power. The poll tax and intimidation had kept them from the polls in the South, and almost total indifference by Democrats and Republicans to the plight of blacks in the north discouraged many from voting.

The Democrat Roosevelt's victory over the Republican Hoover in 1932 took place during the onset of the Depression, and many whites were just about as badly off as blacks. The depression shifted the balance of power toward the poor by creating such a large pool of poor and unemployed, especially in urban centers, that the politicians had to woo them as never before in America. It also created a labor-backed Democratic Party to remain in the White House from 1932 until 1952.

# SOLFA 3

*mi*

WHEN WE FIRST moved to the tenement on 1448 Fulton Street, I started hanging out on St. Andrews Place, which was a little one-block-long street half way around the block from where we lived. We could see St. Andrews Place from our back window over the lower garages of Sheffield Farms where they kept the horses and wagons that delivered milk. The houses on St. Andrews Place were better and each had a stoop of about five steps. Mr. Greaves, the father of one of my classmates, actually owned the three-apartment brick building that he lived in. He was a post office clerk. Mr. Edmonds, who rented an apartment in the building next door, worked on the garbage trucks for the Department of Sanitation. These were considered good jobs among blacks in those days. I knew the kids on the block because we all went to P. S. 93, which was just two blocks away. Among the kids on the block, about seven of them were from Barbadian backgrounds. They readily accepted me. I was about 11 and they were around my age. I was soon hanging out on St. Andrews Place every day—most of the time playing ball.

Just about that time, we all joined Boy Scout Troop 263 at St. Phillips, an Episcopal church which was popular among the neighborhood kids because it had a large drum and bugle corps. I couldn't afford a uniform, but miraculously, the next week I found four one-dollar bills lying on the sidewalk one day. My mother added a dollar or two and bought my unofficial uniform, which was acceptable and cost much less than the official uniform. Of course the Boy Scout troops in those days were segregated but that was not a consideration.

Wednesday night was scout meeting. Every meeting we worked on merit badges in such subjects as first aid, semaphore code (with two flags), knot tying and nature. There would also be a formation in the basement of the church, and each scout belonged to a patrol. There were camp songs to learn and sometimes your patrol would have close order drill in the confined space. There was always a certain amount of "cutting up" that kept things from being too serious. I think I got from Tenderfoot as far as Second Class.

My first summer in the troop I was sent by the Fresh Air Fund to the official Boy Scout camp called Ten Mile River in upstate New York. It was a great new experience. Our troop stayed together in one cabin, but we were mixed among all the activities of the huge camp. We awoke to the bugle playing "reveille" and went to bed with "taps." We went on nature hikes, water sports, rattlesnake hunts (we bagged a huge one), and there was an enormous weekend campfire where hundreds of scouts sang camp songs and performed skits. It was impressive and enjoyable.

During the rest of the year, the troop took swimming classes at the still segregated Carlton Avenue YMCA. Further downtown a huge YMCA admitted only whites. We didn't wear bathing suits. But the main attraction of Troop 263 was the drum and bugle corps. We had close to 100 drummers and buglers, and they made a very impressive showing on parade. I was a good bugler and headed one of the platoons. The biggest day was Memorial Day, when the parade moved up Bedford

Avenue to Eastern Parkway and on to Prospect Park. George Nixon, our drum major, created excitement for the crowds as he shuffled, trucked and gyrated and threw his spinning baton two or three stories high and caught it coming down—sometimes behind his back—as he led the band. The three or four top Boy Scout troops all had colorful drum majors who could really strut.

After about three years of this, an order came down that the drum majors could no longer shuffle, dance, or throw their batons at the Memorial Day Parade, because it was a parade to honor the dead of World War I. This took a lot of the excitement out of the parade.

But all in all, what with going to school, playing ball and games on St. Andrews Place, going to scout meetings, band practice, shining shoes on Saturdays for extra money, and my chores at home, I was pretty busy.

Two years later, we kids on St. Andrews Place decided to go camping on our own (none of that scoutmaster stuff for us). We planned a ten-day trip to Tibbets Brook Park in Westchester County, which at the time seemed like going to another state. We borrowed some old "pup and wall" tents from the troop and planned and packed for the trip over several days.

The morning we left, we all resembled pack mules, with pots, frying pans, bedrolls, clothes, canteens, and towels hanging everywhere over our backpacks. We also had all our food for the ten days on our backs. Somehow I don't think that our parents were fully aware that we had not made any previous arrangements and that we were going to camp on just about any ground we could find. They thought we were going to a designated place. They said goodbye, and we started out—a rag-tag band in piecemeal uniforms, with packs almost as big as we were, and drawing curious glances from on-lookers as we made our way down the street to the I.R.T. subway on Eastern Parkway.

We put our nickels in the turnstile, boarded the train and rode—and rode and rode. Finally the train came up out of the ground to the elevated and we were in what looked like the country (but, in reality, was the upper Bronx). We began to cheer at the sight of the woods and trees. The train rumbled to the last stop. We hooked up our gear and walked downstairs. We saw some buses marked Westchester County, but paid no attention to where the buses were going. We asked somebody for the direction to Tibbets Brook Park, and proceeded to walk what turned out to be a seven-mile hike with full gear on our backs to Tibbets Brook Park in Westchester County.

By the time we got there (we didn't know that camping was not allowed in the park), we were so tired that we just dropped at the first clearing we could find. We dropped right in the middle of a gang of yellow jackets, which, we discovered, built their nests in the ground. Those yellow jackets were buzzing everywhere, but we didn't (couldn't) move. After a long rest, we moved over a few yards and began clearing the ground and pitching tents before nightfall. That night we sat around the fire joking. During the next ten days, we only went into the park proper for water, ate only the food we packed, kept a low profile for forest rangers, and had a great time. We did the same thing the following year.

When I was about 11, we moved from 1342 Fulton Street to 548 Franklin Avenue to a building that was a former Salvation Army headquarters and then the home of the Brooklyn branch of the Refuge Church of Christ, Bishop C. Lawson (Founder).

My father got half the rent off by serving as building superintendent. We got to know some of the kids of the congregation and went to Sunday school and sometimes church there. Living in the building, we were exposed (whether we wanted to be or not) to the best in Gospel music and Evangelical preaching all day long on Sundays, and for several evenings during the week for almost two years.

The church was against drinking, smoking, dancing, even going to the movies, but when the music started it would have everyone dancing in their seats—or in the aisle—and glorious sounds would be heard. As things got heated, several had their own individual steps and movements that made very interesting watching.

Just about the time that the folks were aroused to fever pitch, a big dark skinned woman named Sister Rock, who always wore black, and was the reputed star of these joyous moments, would suddenly rise and go into a slow spin. As she picked up momentum—arms flailing and head weaving—you got the feeling of a tornado about to happen. Needless to say, everyone gave her a wide circle. More than one member found out that sitting too close to Sister Rock could be downright dangerous. Only newcomers sat near her, except when the church was packed, and those that had to sit near her kept a wary eye out. More than one chair literally went by the boards as a result of Sister Rock's "gettin' happy."

I remember one night an unsuspecting man walked into the church and went and sat right next to Sister Rock. He was probably a newcomer or someone just coming in out of the cold. The music started up and things started getting heated, but the man was so tired that he had fallen fast asleep as soon as he sat down, and he never woke up until the service was over and he was put out. Most of us thought she could wake a dead man.

On another Sunday she was feeling so good that when she went into her usual spin, she added a couple more turns—got dizzy—lost her balance and on the way down, she broke two chairs. She rolled over and got up talking in tongues—and the congregation made a joyful noise unto the Lord.

My mother had taken in a roomer, a Mr. Goodfriend and his "wife," who had a small bedroom on the second floor and were allowed kitchen privileges. Mr. Goodfriend was from Philadelphia and had a dapper appearance. He seemed to be in his late thirties, wore spats and a derby, carried a walking cane and kept himself unusually neat.

He seemed to be a mild and pleasant man. We liked him. His "wife" was a full-bodied handsome woman who was rather quiet and worked every day. He moved in about four months before we moved from 548 Franklin Avenue. I don't remember what forced us out of the house, but after a year or so living there, we had to move. Mr. Goodfriend agreed to move with us, so Momma found an apartment that was much better than anything we'd had before in a building with a stoop in front. We lived two flights up and were very proud to live in the building, although, to the average person, it wasn't anything special.

As luck would have it, we only lived there two months. Mr. Goodfriend, for some reason or other, decided to move. This left us in the awkward position of not being able to pay the rent and we had to get out.

From there we moved to a dilapidated tenement building at 1448 Fulton Street. This landed us on Fulton Street for the second time.

No matter how poor the dwelling was, Momma insisted on a clean house. Evelyn and I took turns washing and drying the dishes each evening. I scrubbed the kitchen linoleum every Saturday and emptied the garbage every day. I washed the windows and helped in the spring and fall cleaning.

When we started school I was in kindergarten and my sister was in first grade. When the school examined her, as was the custom in those days, she was found to have a slight heart murmur. Although she was never sick and in fact a healthy child, she was excused from gym classes and avoided all strenuous activities. Her main chore was babysitting our little brother Will who was five years younger. She would carry the house key around her neck. Some children at school wore a piece of garlic on a string around their necks to ward off colds or disease, and school kids were checked regularly for head lice.

Evelyn also had her list of duties, and later Will, as he got older. We three kids shared the same bed until Evelyn got too old to sleep with boys (about six or seven). Will and I shared the same bed until

I left for the Army. From about age eight or nine, I spent most of my time in the street playing. I came home mainly to eat and sleep.

Evelyn and I shared some mutual friends, but I hardly knew Will at all, although we slept in the same bed. A four-year spread in age in those days was like a generation. As a young teenager, I remember trying to boss my brother around till one day he picked up a clothes iron and held it over his head. Well, that was the end of that. It wasn't until after the war that we began to really know each other.

We were all good-looking, healthy, strong kids, and were very proud and conscious of our appearance. I kept a Sunday suit, and our clothes were generally clean and neat. The Burgie family was a poor but handsome bunch, and they cut a neat path when they stepped out.

Upon graduation from high school in 1941, the five black boys who graduated in our large class were the only ones not given jobs. This, even though the war was on in Europe and America was going full blast supplying the Allies. About a month and a half after graduation, the five of us were summoned by the school to go to the summer home of Mayor Fiorello La Guardia to be given jobs. We got dressed in our best and took the subway out to Queens and were met by a limousine from the Mayor's office, which drove us to the mayor's summer residence. We met the mayor, and also a committee of black leaders, and were given jobs as apprentices in the Fifth Avenue Coach Co. that ran the double decker buses through Manhattan.

It was many years later, while doing a research project that I discovered that this group of blacks included Adam Clayton Powell, and that this was part of a settlement that was reached between the Harlem community and the bus company after prolonged harassment, such as throwing rocks through the windows of moving buses.

The starting pay was 55 cents per hour (22 dollars a week) with a five-cent-an-hour raise every three months for the first year. It was the best job of any that black kids in the neighborhood had. I was just short of 17 when I graduated, so I claimed to be 18 to be old enough for the job. A few months later I witnessed a line-up of the first black bus drivers ever hired by the company.

My first "job" had been at the age of 11. I built a little shoeshine box and shined shoes on Nostrand Avenue on Saturdays for my spare money right through high school. When we moved to 1448 Fulton Street I was 12 and started shining shoes at Sheffield Farms, only a half a block from my house. The milkmen, who delivered milk to homes in their horse-drawn wagons, would end their mornings by writing up their orders in a long room that had tables and benches. Some of the men would let me shine their shoes. They usually gave me a dime. You didn't make much money, but at least you were indoors.

When we moved to 1549 Fulton Street when I was 14, I started shining shoes on 42nd Street and 8th Avenue in Manhattan. I usually made less than a dollar a day at first. A shine was five cents but you hoped for a dime. I would hide my shoeshine box in the orange crate that I used for a seat, so that nobody I knew would see me (I was embarrassed about being a shine boy), and I would take the A train from Brooklyn to 42nd Street in Manhattan on Saturdays when it was not too cold or rainy. The cops were always chasing us. Most of the shoe-shiners were grown men, even gray haired.

Sometimes the cops would come around in plain clothes ahead of the paddy wagon. I kept a sharp lookout for them, but they caught me once. They would sneak up on you and grab the box. You're not going to leave your box, so you follow it into the paddy wagon. When the wagon got full, you were taken to a local jail and all were crowded into a couple of large cells. The cells were filled with bums and drunks, and there was a wide-open toilet in the cell. The worst smell I ever experienced up to that time was when one of those old winos took a crap in the toilet. The whole place stank. Everybody was hollering. The outraged men began banging on the bars, saying all sorts of things. "Let me out of this fucking hole!" "That motherfucker must have been eating shit for his shit to smell that bad!" "That son of a bitch has got to be dead for his shit to smell like that!" This went on for a while until the stench dissipated. After about three hours, our names were called. We went before the magistrate, our boxes were returned, and we were released. It was my only time behind bars. I was about 15 years old. I went home with hardly any money that day, but I never told my mother about it.

Growing up, I was always the little guy. Being a year ahead of myself in school, most of my friends were one or two years older, but I managed to take pretty good care of myself. I never had a real fight in my life, but I was a pretty good southpaw boxer. I also had the prettiest sister for blocks around, so the guys handled me with kid gloves. Evelyn was a soft-spoken, quiet, good girl with a beautiful face and figure, and I guess all the boys hoped that they would marry her when they grew up, and I would be their brother-in-law.

The five feet six inches I ended up with came later rather than earlier. Of course, anybody over six feet tall in those days was considered practically a freak and all the tall girls would walk all drooped over to make themselves appear shorter.

At 16, I drifted away from the St. Andrews Place guys and started hanging out with a group that met regularly at Dave and Mike Roberts' house on Albany Avenue. Their parents had a new "combination" record player and their modest apartment was our headquarters. We sat around, played cards, and danced the linoleum thin just about nightly. Their mother never seemed to mind our presence. We formed a dancing club called "Des Marquis," a name we got from some of the guys who said it was French nobility. Everybody called us "de monkeys."

It was the big band era of 1940 and we mainly "cut a rug" in the living room. We often went to the Savoy ballroom in Manhattan on Sunday nights. The Savoy had a special price of 39 cents before 8 o'clock, and we would often have to run at top speed from the 135th Street subway stop to 140th and Lenox Avenue to make it there before 8 o'clock. We saw all the big bands there: Lucky Millinder, Count Basie, Andy Kirk, Jimmy Lunceford, Chick Webb, Charlie Barnett, Tommy Dorsey with Frank Sinatra, the Savoy Sultans, and we danced and danced. (Getting your wet tie to untie after a sweaty night of dancing required a pretty good tugging.)

The bathrooms were thick with smoke, mainly from the musicians smoking marijuana. None of us kids bothered with the stuff. We'd sneak in a pint of wine and sip it from time to time, but no hard stuff. From age 16, weekends were usually spent at one of the dance halls in Brooklyn or Manhattan or at a St. Peter Claver basketball game and dance, mixed in with a movie.

When I was about 16, I got a job cleaning the floor and straightening up in a small hairdressing parlor that was run by Mrs. Jemmott, an old friend of my mother's. I think she paid me about two dollars a week. It was just a so-so job and I was grossly underpaid for the amount of work I did. But I hardly noticed it because one of the three hairdressers at the shop was also the Queen of Sheba. I mean I really fell for this chick. She was a medium brown-skinned, sloe-eyed gal with a dimple and a way of looking at you out of the corner of her eyes that was devastating. I estimate that she was about in her mid-twenties at the time. Her name was Nancy.

Up to then, my association with girls in general had been limited to a girl named Catherine who was among a group we visited regularly on Pacific Street. I was 13and she was14. She was supposed to be my girl, and once in a while I'd actually kiss her on her cheek, but that was all there was.

In those days, you didn't fool around with a girl that you really thought anything of. Also, I went to an all-boys vocational high school. Many of the high schools were not co-ed. I got my first real "piece" from a girl who was a tomboy and also what you would call "easy." Sometimes the guys would trade stories about this girl. There would be one in every neighborhood. We called them "goody girls." But the girl you liked enough to be called your girl, you wouldn't even imagine making out with her.

But back to Nancy. I was now 16 and really stuck on her. I thought about her often during the course of a day, and the big day was when I went to the beauty parlor to clean. While scrubbing the floor or emptying the trash baskets, I'd steal a glance at her as she worked on some woman's hair. She would say hello and exchange a few words, or send me out for a Coke, but other than that, she was reserved, although sometimes she would give me a nice smile. Once or twice while I was cleaning near her, our eyes would meet, which would send cold shivers down my back. Sometimes at night I would dream about her.

This went on for a few weeks until I came in one day and Nancy wasn't there. They told me she had taken a job at a bigger hairdresser across town. Boy, did I feel bad! The next week I got out my shine box and went back to 42nd Street in Manhattan.

Almost 40 years later, I went to see the movie *Here We Go Again* and saw an actress play the part of Sidney Poitier's wife. I was dumbstruck and fell in love with her on sight. A couple of years later I was introduced to her at a party. A little while later, it dawned on me that the reason I was so taken by this woman was because she looked like Nancy, whom I hadn't seen since she left the beauty parlor in my adolescence.

I never thought much about my first name until I was in my teens. It wasn't until I established some mobility as a young man that people, especially Jews, would inquire as to how I acquired the name Irving. I had heard of one or two boys of West Indian descent with that name, but any person outside of the West Indies with the first name Irving was absolutely Jewish. In the West Indies it was Irving, and in some cases spelt with the vowel "*e*" at the end (Irvine). I did a bit of research on this and found that Irving was originally an English name, hence its use among the colonies of Great Britain in the Caribbean.

Jews sometimes adopted the name as the anglicized version of
Israel. When Jews anglicized their names as a means of identifying
with the cultures of the countries they lived in, mainly to avoid
discrimination, they were likely to carry the first initial of the name.
That's a possible explanation for its popularity among Jews.

Despite being kidded once in a while, I always liked the name,
and being black, I felt it added to my style.

The question of color has been a complex one in the black society,
made complex by the definition and standards of American society.
A black man, a colored man, a Negro in the United States has been
generally designated as one who has any black blood, even a drop.
Mulattoes had half-black and half-white blood; quadroons, one-quarter
black blood; and octoroons, one-eighth black blood. After that, in most
cases, there was an assumed crossover into the white race. There were
also many gradations in between, developed through miscegenation
generally. For example, if two light-skinned blacks (octoroons, that
is, blacks with one-eighth black blood) married and had a child,
the child still would be called a mulatto because both parents were
black—however, the percentage of black blood in the child could vary
tremendously. The child would still be called black, but would have
only one-eighth black blood.

During the early days of World War II, a regiment of Puerto Rican
soldiers was formed. They were kept together, because the military was
at odds as to how to deploy them. Puerto Ricans, who run the color
spectrum, from black to white, are all registered as white. The story is
told that when the regiment was lined up and it was requested that all
white soldiers step forward, the whole regiment took a step forward. All
Puerto Ricans were designated as white, regardless of their skin color.

As a racially identifying factor, "Negro" is not used anywhere in the
world except in the United States. The white power structure created
a preference of light-skinned blacks over dark-skinned blacks from

an early period. The mulatto and quadroon, in high degree, became the mistresses of their masters, and most of the lighter skinned slaves became the preferred house Negroes—maids, chambermaids, servants, butlers, cooks, yard boys, nursemaids, baby sitters and groomers, while those who were dark skinned worked primarily in the fields. The fact that some of these house Negroes were related by blood to their masters also improved their position in the slave hierarchy. This type of color preference permeated all forms of black life.

The prospect of a slave owner, an overseer, or other white functionary, spawning illegitimate mulatto offspring among as many concubines as he desired, in a proximity as close as his own household, had to be a cause for concern in the social structure of the legitimate family of the day. Surely, this triangle must have been the source of at least some degree of havoc and uncertainty in the mind of the celebrated "Southern Belle." The practice of miscegenation involved the whole spectrum of Southern society, from the lowest echelon of white worker to the noblest families. No less a figure than George Washington, the father of our country, was also the father of several mulatto children and is reputed to have had several black concubines. Ironically, Washington is a rather common surname in black circles, but I have never met a white Washington to date, though some may exist.

After the Civil War, many masters sent their illegitimate offspring to the newly established schools for blacks and Indians, such as Hampton, Tuskegee Institute, and Howard University. Also all of the pictorial and advertising images were white: Madame Walker became rich with hot combs and pomades that straightened black women's hair to make it "like white people's." And they sold all sorts of creams that were supposed to make your complexion lighter. Only "high yallers" were hired in the For White Customers Only Cotton Club chorus line in Harlem and at Connie's Inn. It was later disclosed that a black woman as light as Lena Horne almost didn't make the Cotton Club line because she was considered a shade too dark.

If the blacks, who were brought to America as slaves, could have their color-race altered through miscegenation over a period of some three hundred years, can you imagine what took place in Spain, which the Moors conquered and held power in for eight hundred years until they were finally defeated by Ferdinand and Isabella in the year 1492, the same year that Columbus discovered America?

There were also invasions of Italy and other European Mediterranean countries by Africans in various epochs in history. Ethnologically speaking, the deep brunette and "dark" complexion of the Euro-Mediterranean peoples are directly related to their proximity to Africa (and I don't mean the heat).

During the civil rights drive of the 1960s, the previously favored fair-skinned type was superseded by the dark-skinned Sidney Poitier as the prototype in black films. When private employers had to meet government quotas in the hiring of blacks to qualify for government contracts, they went out of their way to hire the most highly visible blacks they could find.

The black color spectrum had, in a way, come full cycle.

When jobs that required contact with the public were first given to blacks, those of light complexion were usually chosen over the darker ones. When a black woman was used to advertise a product or connote any positive values of black womanhood, a light-skinned woman was always used. By generations of favoritism, light skinned blacks began to show discernible patterns of superior buying power, education, and upbringing.

The black person of dark complexion was only characterized and portrayed as a buffoon. In cartoons, he was always depicted as jet black with a white ring around his mouth. Bert Williams, the highest ranked star on the white vaudeville circuit, was reputed to be a comic genius. He was a light skinned black man whose background was West Indian. However, celebrated as he was, he appeared always on stage as a black buffoon. This was a source of great anguish to Williams, as his biographers later revealed. When the movies came around, such black stars as Mantan Morland and Stepin Fetchit carried on this stereotype.

Marcus Garvey coined the phrase "Black is beautiful" in the 1920s, and for the first time, on a large scale, many blacks became proud of their blackness. But it was not until the civil rights movement of the 1950s that the "Black is beautiful" concept really penetrated the rank and file of the black masses. And it was of their own doing.

Many black men desired light skinned brides because of the projected "Caucasian image" and for the fact that, all things being equal, those women stood a better chance in the job market. Black women's desire was exactly the same. And they felt that, down the line, their children would have lighter skins and "non-kinky" straight hair, thus increasing their chances of "making it."

This was a highly prevalent theme during the 1920s and 1930s and vestiges of it have persisted.

During the 1960s and 1970s, as the black drive toward education manifested itself in better jobs, in more diverse professions, there have been a number of interracial unions particularly among professionals. The black family's ideal, though, still welcomes a qualified black suitor or bride.

The black community always had a flair for color and style, even among the poorest. Over the years, the style would go from peg bottoms to stovepipes to bellbottoms in slacks, from a Windsor knot to a half Windsor in ties. Many people claim that the top fashion designers used to go to places like the Savoy and the Golden Gate to get ideas. Every year, I'd save up a little shoeshine money for my Easter suit. One particular Easter, I decided to use my blue shadow-stripe jacket from a previous suit and have some new pants made. The style then was peg bottom and wide at the knee. Some guys wore those "ankle chokers" at 14 inches, but I was more conservative and held mine at 15- to 15 ½-inch ankle with a 28-inch knee. Some guys had a 14-inch ankle and ballooned out to 32 inches at the knee, which made them look like something out of "Arabian Nights." When I was 15 and 16, only "squares" bought their clothes from clothing stores. Practically all of us kids had our suits and pants made to order. The Jews had a monopoly in the tailoring business, and they would fit you and make a suit for about $20. You went and picked out the material and all. And, man, those cats could sew! My favorite tailor and one of the cheapest was Edelman's on Myrtle Avenue in Brooklyn.

I stopped in at the Knox hat shop and bought one of those fine wide brims where the rim broke at just the right angle. In those days, you really weren't dressed without a hat. To contrast my dark blue shadow stripe jacket, I chose a piece of light cloth, sort of beige with just a dash of orange in it, and had it made up to my specifications. I then went down to Flagg Bros. and bought a pair of brown brogues, a very heavy looking dress shoe with a thick sole. The year before, the style was called knobs—a shoe that came up almost to a long point and stuck up in the air a little, a bit like a pair of Turkish slippers.

With these tan brogues, dark-blue, shadow-stripe, single-breasted jacket and light-beige pegs, and my Knox wide-brim hat, I was as "ready as Freddie" for Easter.

While I was walking across the corner of Fulton and Nostrand, a convertible filled with white people stopped for a red light. They looked at me and then they looked at each other—then they burst into convulsive laughter. It made me annoyed as hell as I looked back at them rolling down the street, still laughing like crazy. I stood there trying to figure out what they thought was so damn funny. I looked behind me, but nobody was there. But I just felt they could not have been laughing at me, sharp as I was. Yeah, like the guys around the block would say, "I was sharp as a rat's turd." That meant sharp at both ends.

If it's true that we acquire our virtues in the course of growing up, it's also true that we develop our vices as well. As an adult I find it difficult to remember people's names, and I definitely blame it on a practice I acquired as an apprentice mechanic with the Fifth Avenue Coach Co.

Being a month from 17 years old when I graduated from Brooklyn Automotive High School, I was thrown in with a group of much older and experienced men, predominantly Irish, who had come up the hard way and were formerly the mechanics on the trolley cars that preceded the buses. One black fellow named Brownie worked in the body shop, where I was apprenticed.

My first job, which lasted the year of my apprenticeship, was to supply the men with nuts, bolts, screws, washers, or whatever they needed to do the particular job they were assigned. I would make the rounds regularly to the men in the body shop, and I got on pretty well with them. I think this position was created because the shop bosses didn't quite know what to do with me.

My immediate foreman was an old-timer named John Wolff who, like many of the others, had worked many years for the company. When I wrote out an order from one of the workers, I would bring it to Wolff's stand-up desk for signature and inspection, then go to the supply room and give the man in the supply room the order. In a few minutes he would return with the order in various boxes, and I would then carry the boxes to the crew working on the buses. Just having arrived at my 17th birthday, I was the youngest person in the entire company (I had lied that I was 18 to get the job). There were some young men in their mid-twenties but the older men predominated.

Most of the men called each other by their last or first names. Being so young, I was perplexed as to how I should address these men, especially the foreman, and the two or three minor bosses who moved to and from the office. I finally dreamed up a system where I addressed most of the more friendly workers by their first or last names. The foreman and others, I never addressed at all. If I had anything to say to them, I just ran up to them, stepped in front of them, and started talking. I did this for the entire year of my apprenticeship even though I had to get Wolff's signature for every order, which was several times a day.

Mostly, the men in the body shop were good-natured, especially the two crews that worked on reinforcing the chassis. Joe, a young Irishman; McGuire, an old Irishman; and Gus (real name Gustavus Adolphus von Hecht), a blond, handsome bright young man of German descent about 25, who commuted from New Jersey.

McGuire was good-natured, had a marvelous sense of wit and could at will spin off engaging yarns full of Irish folklore and life. His description of a particular Irish wake was hilarious. It was during this time that I began to pick up the similarity of the Irish brogue with the West Indian dialect. Later on I did some research and found that the original overseers of the slaves in the Caribbean were mostly indentured Irish and Scots. Many of the original overseers were serving time as political prisoners, thieves, murderers, deserters, and especially debtors. A particular account of a Scottish rebellion reveals that after the British crushed the rebellion, the prisoners were lined up, every tenth prisoner shot dead, and the rest packed up and sent off to Barbados.

I found myself spending more and more time in the place where McGuire and his crew worked on the bus. I told a few stories myself. They liked me very much. They worked in and under the bus so that you could hardly see who was inside the bus working unless you came up close. I found myself beating it in a hurry when a boss or foreman approached.

Each job was timed in man-hours. The reinforced chassis was a 96-hour job, which meant that three shifts worked 24 hours a day for four days. Management and the Transport Workers Union, of which all workers were members, established these standards. On the first day the men would strip the buses with pneumatic hammers with chisel heads. It was a dirty job and the years of accumulated dirt and grime on the bus would fall as the chisel cut the bolt head off. After this, there would be much joking, wisecracking and story telling which could continue into much of the next day. The foreman might pass that way on occasion, but there was no close supervision because the hours were fixed. After a leisurely second day, the crew really went into action by the morning of the third day. Dirt was flying, hammers banging, pneumatic bolt tighteners screaming, and men taking care of business. By the afternoon of the fourth day, the bus was ready to be inspected. A test driver came over, wheeled it out of the body shop, and another bus pulled into the spot the first one just left vacant. There were literally hundreds of buses that got this service, so the flow of buses, jokes, stories, and pranks never ended.

I was a victim of a classic prank soon after arriving. Sometimes, when a piece of equipment or tool was not available in the body shop stockroom, I was sent to other stockrooms to look for it. Someone requisitioned a skyhook, and I went to the stockroom to get it. The stockroom clerk sent me to the engine department. The engine department sent me to the paint department. The paint department sent me four flights down to the sub-basement where they suggested yet another department. After about an hour of going up and down stairs, it finally occurred to me that there was no such tool as a skyhook. When I got back to my floor, the laugh was on me for the rest of the day.

Whenever I tried to project or assert any knowledge of anything, McGuire would remind me that I "hadn't even stopped pissin' yellow yet" and I was trying to tell him something. I was told this enough times to believe that by the time I was fully mature, my urine would lose its yellow color and turn white. But, as I observed it through the years, it remained yellow.

If you really wanted to get somebody's dander up, you would accuse him of "making it" after work with "Annie," which was a pet name for the local Broadway and 135th Street "character." She was a sort of neighborhood bag woman, a white woman in her late forties, unkempt and probably demented.

Our hours were 8 AM to 4:30 PM daily for five days a week. Lunch was from 12:30 to 1 PM. (The men elected to take only half an hour for lunch in order to get off at 4:30.) Sometimes we ate at the local diner or often, in nice weather, we would bring our homemade bag lunches outside and sit out on the sidewalk along Broadway, in front of a Buick showroom. Invariably, as we sat in the sun eating our lunches, someone would spot Annie coming down Broadway. She would start running toward us with her dress held high and wearing no panties.

The men would scatter and create a lot of excitement, much to the delight of Annie. She would drop her dress and then continue on down the street, and the men would go back to eating their lunches.

Many of the older guys were criticized quietly by the younger men who called them "eager beavers" because, not having much to do with their lives, they always showed up for work as much as an hour early. They would sit around preparing their tools, changing clothes, having coffee, or just plain sitting, till the 8 AM whistle blew to start work. The younger guys were running and hustling to punch the clock by 8. The company kept strict time and did not tolerate any chronic lateness.

Sometimes the younger men would jokingly accuse an older guy of having shares in the company. Smoking was forbidden in the building, even in the toilets, and most of the young smokers, myself included, would sneak a smoke in the toilet. Many of the older men satisfied their nicotine craving by chewing tobacco.

Lloyd Jackson was the neighborhood bully. And he had a reputation. He was known to have been in innumerable brawls and it was rumored that he had even killed a couple of people. He and his younger brother had gone to P.S. 93 and they were well known and feared all over town. He and his boys hung out at the poolroom on Fulton Street where I often passed on my way to my friends on Albany Avenue. One Sunday afternoon I was dressed in my best and passing the poolroom. Lloyd was standing out front talking to a former friend of mine, Bill Young, who was now a part of Lloyd's gang. I had been on casual speaking terms with Lloyd and he stopped me and asked me to give him a quarter. I told him I had no quarter. Then he asked for a dime, then a nickel, and I gave the same answer. Then he asked me for two cents.

Now here was the baddest cat in Brooklyn—standing in front of me, asking for two cents. I don't know to this day what came over me, but my eyes narrowed, my face tensed and must have taken on a look of sheer outrage. I had nothing really to do with it. My body was not reacting to the signals of my mind. But my face remained fixed in that snarling, outraged expression. I was sending signals to my face, but it would not respond. I even whispered to my face—"Don't you know that little you are standing here snarling in the face of the baddeeesssttt Negro in Brooklyn?" I even began to tremble a little. For what seemed the longest few seconds, nothing happened. Then Lloyd, looking at my face in disbelief, shouted: "Why, you little bastard, don't you look at me like that. Why, I'll kill you, you little motherfucker."

He reached for me, and I backed away. He then ran to kick me in the rear, and I turned to avoid the kick. Bill Young grabbed him and held him. Lloyd continued to scream epithets at me as Bill held him. With two or three other of his boys that I knew looking on, I walked up the street. My face was flushed, my blood was boiling, and I felt a great humiliation.

For a week, I plotted ways of killing Lloyd Jackson. I thought and thought about it until after a while the whole idea began to wear thin. Finally I let it go. But I never saw Lloyd Jackson again. There was a rumor about a year later that he had gotten the chair for killing a couple of people, but about that time I was getting ready to go into the army.

It was during my apprentice year in 1941 that I took my first paid-for lessons in music. My friend Lloyd Edwards, who had graduated from Brooklyn Automotive High School with me and was working upstairs in the paint shop, was taking saxophone lessons at a commercial music

studio on Nostrand Avenue in Brooklyn. I liked to sing to myself and
fancied myself as a romantic singer playing a guitar, so I took guitar
lessons. This was just a rudimentary, commercial course in picking
out popular melodies of the day, but I took to it and learned to pick out
several melodies without learning any chords or bars before I stopped
lessons.

I could pick out the melodies to such ditties as "Goodbye, Momma,
I'm Off to Yokohama" and "Apple Blossom Time," popular songs just
about the time of the US entry into World War II. I was lent a guitar
to practice with and returned it when I stopped going for lessons. It
would be another seven years before I held a guitar again.

# SOLFA 4

*fa*

O N DECEMBER 7, 1941, Pearl Harbor was attacked and the United States went to war against Germany, Italy, and Japan.

The first American hero of World War II was created that day, when Dorey Miller, a black sailor on board an American warship that was being bombed and torpedoed by enemy planes took over the gun position of a fallen comrade and continuously returned fire on the diving Japanese planes. For this act of bravery, Dorey Miller was awarded the Navy Cross. Ironically, Miller was a mess attendant, a steward, the only position open to a black man in the US Navy at the start of the war. And until World War II, there were no blacks at all in the marines.

The following months were times of great anxiety in America. The whole country mobilized for war. Millions of men were drafted, and blacks, for the first time since World War I, were actually invited to work in defense plants. I mean everybody had a job—even women. A popular song of the day was "Rosie the Riveter."

The following spring my sister Evelyn was recruited by the
government to work as a clerk in Washington, D.C., even though blacks
could not drink a Coca-Cola in drug stores in the nation's capital. A few
months before Sis left, a young fellow, who lived a few blocks away, who
had just joined the Merchant Marines, used to drop in to visit her when
he was in town. One day the news came back that a German submarine
torpedoed his ship and he was killed. He was the first casualty of the
neighborhood and people took it hard as they looked around and saw
their sons and loved ones preparing to go to war. The boy's mother got
ten thousand dollars from his insurance and she bought a little house.
But she pined over her son. She considered the insurance as a bit of
blood money and in two years she died too.

My mother got a job sewing uniforms for the navy. My parents were
just about estranged by this time and my father got a job as a building
superintendent in an apartment building. He only came home every
couple of weeks or so.

The following summer I took my two-week vacation (my first time
out of New York State). I went to visit my father's home in Shipman,
Virginia, and then on to Richmond, and then I visited my sister in
Washington. My co-worker, Lloyd Edwards, was with me and we stood
in front of Union Station with our bags for a long time before a black
man came by and told us that we had to go around to the side of the
station to pick up a colored cab.

In the summer of 1942 the draft had gotten down to the 18-
year-olds, and I had decided to join the Army Air Corps rather
than wait to be drafted. If you volunteered, you were allowed to
pick your branch of service. At the time, the air corps sounded a
bit more glamorous than the infantry. They had established the 99th
Pursuit Squadron, an all-black unit of the air corps, at Tuskegee,
Alabama, and I fancied myself at the controls of a P-38 fighter,
flying off into the wild blue yonder, so I got my mother's reluctant
consent to join.

Looking back on my childhood growing up in the tenements of Bedford-Stuyvesant in Brooklyn, I realized how lucky I was. When I was eight, I was running from a playmate and I made a wrong turn down the basement steps and ran into a stone wall that put a huge bump on my forehead that kept me out of school for a week. During that week I was playing ball against the stoop and the ball went into the street. I ran to retrieve it. As I turned to go back, two cars raced by me at the same time, one in front of me, and one behind. They were speeding, and the wind that they created rippled my clothing. They both passed within a couple of inches of hitting me. I didn't tell my mother.

A little while later an older kid from the block, whose nickname was "Hard Rock," induced me to take a ride down from the roof of our building on the top of a dumbwaiter. Our weight started the dumbwaiter down and as it picked up speed the rope burned our fingers. The rope broke and the dumbwaiter was in a free fall the last couple of floors. It hit the cellar and broke up under us. The iron rope pulleys in the roof were old and rusty, but they did not fall on us. A crowd gathered in the basement, among them my mother. But she was too frightened to beat me. We only suffered a couple of rope burns on our fingers.

Another time we skipped the el (sneaked on without paying). We wanted to go in the other direction, so we decided to cross the tracks rather than go to the next double station. In crossing the track I stumbled slightly, and just managed to clear the third rail on my way over. Not a scratch!

One hot day, we skipped the el to Coney Island for a swim. There were three buoys leading from shore to the deep water. Many of the kids swam out to the third buoy, a distance of about fifty feet of deep water. They would rest on the third buoy but there were too many people holding on to the buoy and it was under water. I was too tired to swim back and I started thrashing about helplessly. Luckily, a big

guy out there told the others to get off the buoy. He held onto me until
the buoy was back up. I held onto the buoy until I got my wind back,
then I swam back to shore. Also, in my adolescence, "hitching" on the
back of trolley cars was a favorite pastime. As I prepared to go into
the army, I mused, "Somebody up there likes me"!

Taking a chance is a natural part of the American heritage. There
was more opportunity in a relatively new land like America to move
from one station to another in life than in the older societies that
most immigrants came from. Often it is necessary to take a chance
in order to get to the next step. It is fundamentally American. The
Pilgrims did it—the early settlers of the west did it—the immigrants
did it—Patrick Henry and George Washington did it—Charles
Lindbergh, Admiral Peary, and Amelia Earhart did it—Martin
Luther King Jr. did it. Taking a chance is key in "the pursuit of
happiness."

While I was in high school, I learned to operate a lathe, to use
calipers, and to read micrometers, and I became familiar with such
tools as socket wrenches, open-end wrenches, T-squares, nuts, bolts,
lock washers, screws, and learned the functions of an engine. But at
the bus company there were three general units—the body shop, the
engine shop, and the paint shop. Most of the men only worked in one
of these. I was apprenticed to the body shop, and the gang I worked
with basically installed new steel plates to the lower rear chassis of
the buses being repaired, where they began to wear after thousands
of miles. So, everything I had learned about cars, engines, cylinders,
and carburetors became a memory because each shop performed but
one function. Only two men in the body shop were allowed to chauffeur
the buses in and out of the shop. I did this bodywork for the two years
that I worked for the bus company before I went into the army. The
other workers had been doing the same routine, one bus after another,
sometimes for years. And I was considered lucky to have this job at
the bus company!

Dad, Louis Burgie

Mother, Viola Callender Burgie

Sister, Evelyn Burgie Jenkins

Brother, Will Burgie

Fifth Avenue Bus Co. (1942)

On vacation in Washington, D.C. (1942)

Camp Minisink, Port Jervis, N.Y. (1952)

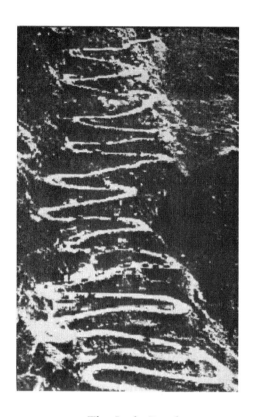

The Ledo Road

Truck convoy on Ledo Road

With Indian troops in
Bombay (1943)

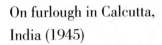

On furlough in Calcutta,
India (1945)

The Company Chapel in North Burma where I first sang

A Christmas card (1944)

A letter to Mom from Burma (1945)

Fort Dix wasn't far from New York, and they gave us passes home at the reception center. I had a fine handwriting and enjoyed writing home and receiving mail. Calling home was out because up till then we never had a phone. At the reception center at Fort Dix, New Jersey, you were kept very busy getting your clothing, uniforms, medical shots, and learning how to fix your bunk, basic hygiene, and orientation. I was made a guide and led groups of recruits around the center. I took the I. Q. test and passed, which made me eligible for officer candidate school, but then I was only 18 and probably looked more like a patrol leader in the Boy Scouts.

And my Boy Scout days did pay off; I was very good at close-order drill and could command a platoon. Uniforms, reveille, bugle calls, hikes, mess kits, canteens and outdoor living, in general, were nothing new to me. As a guide at Fort Dix, I had great fun directing and showing the new recruits how to get their medical shots, uniforms and gear, each day. The food at the reception center was great. You could eat as much as you wanted, within reason, and the table was always full of jam, apple butter, peanut butter and bread. I hadn't remembered encountering apple butter before and I really ate it up.

I filled up to the brim at every meal. After a couple of days, I noticed that I hadn't gone to the toilet, except to urinate. The Army toilets (latrines) were set out in long rows, and there would be maybe seven or eight guys in a row sitting over the holes. I finally sat down once, a little squeamish, but nothing happened. I knew I was running all day and burning up energy but I thought I should have some waste. I had heard that sudden changes in food, location, or water could constipate you, but not that much. I also realized that sharing a heretofore private function with all those other soldiers was contributing greatly to my discomfort. Well, it wasn't until six days after I arrived at the post that my bowels actually moved. Man, was I relieved!

I was on the move from morning till night. Everything was so new and it was my first time really away from home except for camp or vacation. But this was for real. There was a war going on and the papers began giving great accounts of battles raging in North Africa with the German desert fox Rommel and the American General Patton.

The elementary schools I went to in Brooklyn were bi-racial. The high school was predominantly white and the workers at the bus company were 95 percent white. But the army was totally segregated. In each place I went, starting at Fort Dix, the area that you were in was all black except for white non-coms as instructors. Also, at only 18 years old, I was among the youngest wherever I went, as the age limit was 18 to 38. But I had been working with older men at the bus company, so it wasn't a difficult adjustment.

We were housed in barracks with long rows of bunks on each side of an aisle. As part of our orientation we were shown a film on venereal disease that showed women from different parts of the world with all sorts of deformities and growths on their bodies from syphilis, gonorrhea, and other diseases that, I am certain, turned a lot of guys off sex for a while. It was quite disgusting, enough maybe that a few of the guys were turned off forever. But maybe not.

After a couple of weeks of orientation, medical shots and uniforms, I was put in a contingent bound for Jefferson Barracks, Missouri, an air corps basic training center, where they made you into a soldier in six weeks.

At Jefferson Barracks we were housed six to a tent. Only a few of the recruits were from Dix, but we had a tent of young guys. It was around Thanksgiving, and it was getting blustery cold out on the drill fields where we practiced marching drills every day. Sometimes the days were unusually warm and a couple of men would pass out from heat exhaustion on the drill field. The training was rigorous, but not overly so. Our drill corporals and sergeants were all white, down-home boys, who were probably briefed on the handling of black troops. They were careful not to call you "boy," but they were generally no-nonsense and fair in dealing with you.

Most parts of Missouri were segregated and most public places had separate colored-white facilities—the colored in most cases being decidedly inferior. Although there was a large black population in St. Louis, being in a segregated place, I was not anxious to go to town on a pass. I had been raised in Brooklyn, where blacks lived primarily in ghettos, but where there was no overt discrimination.

The days were spent taking short and long hikes or drilling or bivouacking, with occasional obstacle courses, calisthenics, and general orientation. In the evenings you would gab with your tent mates or visit the PX (post-exchange) where you could buy things tax-free. The only time you saw women was at the various counters in the PX.

There was a wood-burning stove in the middle of our tent that gave some warmth, but four feet away from the stove you could hardly feel it. The cots were lined around the walls of the tent, and you dressed almost as warm to go to bed as you did to go outside. Much of the camp aspect of the training I had already done in the Boy Scouts. The main difference was that the scout camp was mostly in summer, and it was more of a game. They took us out on the rifle range and, although I had only fired a small .22 at the amusement park at Coney Island, I scored expert, the highest score.

I only went to town once on a pass. I got back several hours after the curfew and, instead of going to bed, I had to spend a few hours digging a hole in that frozen Missouri clay as punishment.

In the evenings the men wrote home and sometimes received packages with some goodies, like a cake or candy. I didn't have a girlfriend at the time, but I had a crush on my sister's girlfriend, Marie, who was pretty, but three years older than I. I dropped her a line once in a while, along with my sister and brother. I wrote mom fairly regularly.

Right after Christmas our six-week basic training was over, and I guess because I had worked for the bus company, they sent me to

the Holabird Army Ordinance base in Baltimore, Maryland. There
we were introduced to trucks, bulldozers, rollers, graders, and other
heavy equipment. They carried their own support and supply units.
(During the war the Air Force was connected to the army, and called
the Army Air Corps and then the Army Air Force.)

At night, sometimes we would go to the USO in town. College girls
and some from local social organizations would volunteer to assist in
entertaining the soldiers and talking with them. Many soldiers shunned
the USOs and opted for bars and saloons, where they could pick up
women.

After a month at Holabird, I was shipped off by train to Myrtle
Beach, South Carolina, where I was assigned to the 849th Aviation
Engineers Battalion. The outfit was forming in preparation for overseas
duty. It was a battalion trained to build airfields and landing strips. I was
assigned to the motor pool. I was put into the Headquarters and Service
company of the battalion, which had four other companies A, B, C, and
D. Each company operated as an arm of the battalion. A lieutenant
colonel headed the battalion and five captains or first lieutenants were
the company commanders under him. There were probably a dozen
officers in each company, all first or second lieutenants.

All the officers in the battalion were white except the battalion
chaplain Captain Nichols, who was black. We walked past the town
a couple of times on long hikes and bivouacs, but I never asked for
a pass to go to town because South Carolina was very segregated and
the area that black troops were allowed in was so wild that the local
bar was nicknamed "the bucket of blood." I considered the sergeant
of the motor pool a real "Uncle Tom," bucking for stripes in the new
unit. Besides work in the motor pool, we went on the usual hikes, close
order drills, and bivouacs (one night camp-outs). There were plenty of
snakes in the woods of South Carolina.

Just as I had learned a bit about Irish folklore at the bus company in
New York, I began noticing the colorful phrases and "street" language

of blacks in the South. There were many "tall tales" and incidents, among which they said that you could be arrested and charged with "reckless eyeballing" for looking at a white woman in some southern states. To describe a heavy rain, "Man, it's raining like a cow pissing on a flat rock!" If a girl was attractive she was "as pretty as a white mouth mule." On a really cold day "it's colder than the nuts on a brass monkey." In a poker game if a card turned up that threatened your hand, "Oh, oh, lightning struck the shithouse!"

Every three months or so the whole company would be awakened at 5:00 AM and lined up for "short arm inspection" where the medical officer would examine the penis of everyone in the company to detect any venereal diseases.

One of the later emerging disadvantages of being born at home aided by a midwife is that in most cases, the child was not circumcised. During the 1920s, circumcision became routine for male babies born in New York hospitals. Until then, only Jews, because of religious beliefs, had their children circumcised at birth. Many blacks, being born at home, did not become circumcised until after they joined the armed services.

I was an exception, as my mother told me just before I joined the army. In my early years, I was an inveterate thumb-sucker. Momma told me that I sucked my left thumb, and masturbated with my right hand. The constant action of pulling the skin of my penis back from the head naturally circumcised me. When I was examined after joining the army, I was recorded as being circumcised. The medical officer kidded me by pointing out that I must have some Jew in me, being both named Irving and circumcised.

A private's pay was $50 a month, $54 for duty overseas, plus $10 a month for combat duty. This kept us fairly close to the base, especially those of us who had money deducted from our pay and sent home. What you had left was barely beer and cigarette money.

I was in Myrtle Beach about three months when the battalion was put on alert and moved by train to Fort Dix to await boarding a ship. I managed to get a pass to go to Brooklyn for a day, and after that we mostly waited around until one day the outfit boarded a train to New York to a ferry across New York harbor to our ship. One soldier was playing a mournful blues tune on his harmonica, and others were lost in their thoughts, just like in the movies. The next morning the word was out that we were bound for the China-Burma-India Theater, by way of Bombay, halfway around the world.

The ship, the former S.S. America, the largest US passenger ship (renamed the troopship West Point), was a big fast ship and did not have to travel in a convoy to avoid submarines. It just had to zigzag to keep them from aiming their torpedoes. The 8,000 soldiers slept on canvas bunks with iron frames stacked four high, with just enough space between the stacks to get out of bed and dress. Every few feet pipes funneled fresh air in from above. (A contingent of nurses also was on board, but they got roomier sleeping quarters, being officers.)When the weather was good, going up on deck was a great treat. A lot of guys got seasick, but somehow we managed in that cramped space.

You got an eerie feeling during fire drills when you heard the heavy hatches slamming shut all over the ship to cut off sections in case of a hit. We went through a couple of real alarms during the voyage but no hits.

The first stop was three days at Rio de Janeiro, Brazil, to take on supplies and water. We could see the Sugar Loaf Mountain against the skyline, but we were not allowed to go ashore. Next, we headed to another supply stop at Cape Town in South Africa. We couldn't go ashore there either. (Discrimination against blacks was worse in South Africa than in the U.S.). We continued to zigzag up the Indian Ocean and docked at Bombay. The voyage lasted 34 days; on the way I passed my 19th birthday.

In those days most of us knew no more about India than that it was crowded with people, colorful, had a building the Taj Mahal and had someone called Mahatma Gandhi. We disembarked and walked through town toward our staging area. The streets were filled with mostly poor, clearly downtrodden workers, lots of people just standing around—and beggars. Some were blind, or crippled. Many pointed to festering sores on their bodies. Begging seemed to be some kind of art form.

We were warned not to eat any of the food, but some of the men bought some peanuts on the sly. The officer stopped his platoon and reminded them that "those peanuts were fertilized with human shit," which stopped a few jaws from moving. There were all kinds of unfamiliar smells in the air, and bodies were cremated on stacks of wood.

India—when I was there—had more than half a billion people, but it was still a colony of Great Britain (with only 55 million). The Indian Army was part of the allied forces in Southeast Asia. The people were many colors, from fair to very dark. Sikhs, Punjabi, Kashmiri, Hindus, and Sind were just some of the ethnic and religious groups, and the Hindus had a rigid caste system of which the lowest caste, called the "untouchables," had the darkest skin.

Despite the abject poverty on every hand, India possessed an ancient culture and was reputed to have, among its Maharajas, a few of the world's richest men. The food at the staging area was lousy. It seemed that everything was cooked in a palm oil that smelled and tasted awful. After a couple of days, we boarded the first of several trains that took us across India from Bombay to Calcutta. We had to change trains a couple of times because of differences in the gauge (the distance between the rails, which had been standardized in the US for years). From Calcutta we went into north Burma to a big forward staging area called Ledo.

American and British forces were building the Ledo Road to link up with the old Burma Road, because it had been cut off by the Japanese early in the war. The Allies had to fly "over the hump" (the Himalaya Mountains), a risky and costly way to supply the Chinese army under Chiang Kai-Shek. The US Army sent 10,000 black troops to build and maintain the Ledo Road. Although my outfit was attached to the air force, we were put on the Ledo Road project where we remained for the rest of the war. British, American and other allied soldiers were fighting in the jungles ten to twenty miles ahead of us, and the Japanese were being pushed back more and more as the road was being built.

There are two seasons in Burma, wet and dry, and we arrived smack in the middle of the monsoon season. Sometimes it was hard to find anything dry to wear, and in the beginning we used our helmets to wash in. We slowly moved up the crude road that the lead battalions had cut prior to our arrival. In some places it was very rough with a steep cliff on one side. In many places the road weaved through the mountains much as our ship had zigged and zagged through the water to avoid submarines.

We were quartered in white British tents, six to a tent, and slept on portable canvas cots. Everything was rough at first, with mud everywhere. But soldiers generally kept fairly neat bunks—which were inspected periodically. Our first camp was on the thirty-seven mile mark of the rough-hewn road. Each company of the battalion was a couple of miles apart. Our company, H & S (headquarters and service), was about 150 men including kitchen crew, medics, water supply, heavy equipment operators, clerks and mailmen. The staff included a company commander, usually a captain, and about 15 officers. The highest-ranking enlisted man was the First Sergeant, who ran the company, and his staff of sergeants worked and lived among the men, the privates and corporals.

Although most blacks in the South realized that segregation and "separate but equal" deprived them of their rights as American citizens they were still loyal to the United States, and were in turn trusted by the government (which in those days was the principal employer of blacks). Black leaders were continuing to press for civil rights, and the war had a positive effect on bringing people closer together, be it in the work place or the armed forces. Blacks moved up north from the South in large numbers, as they had during World War I. They became a welcome part of the work force in big cities like New York, Chicago, Detroit, Cleveland, and Newark. In those days, America willingly used all of its human resources.

The black 99th Pursuit Squadron and the 92nd Regiment, as combat units of the armed forces, were tremendous morale boosters for all black soldiers—and for the blacks back home. It meant that blacks were moving toward equality in being allowed to put their lives on the line for their country. The 99th shot down 111 enemy planes and destroyed 273 on the ground at a cost of 70 pilots killed in action, and they never lost an American bomber to enemy fighters on escort missions.

Alaska was vulnerable to an attack by the Japanese and the United States Army built the Alcan Highway between March and October in 1942. It linked the mainland to Alaska. It was a tough, harrowing experience. It was 1,600 miles long, and a third of the soldiers and engineers who built the road were black.

General Joseph (Vinegar Joe) Stillwell was the commander in the China-Burma-India Theater, and the Ledo Road later bore his name. Colonel Lewis E. Pick was the officer in charge of the Ledo Road and Lt. Colonel William J. Green was his chief road engineer. The road was started in late 1942 and by the time we arrived in August 1943, Colonel Green had started a 24-hour work schedule with shifts through the night. It was an eerie but strangely beautiful sight at night, as the flaming torches lit up the road and the big D-8 bulldozers cut into the side of the mountain, the light reflecting on the shining black faces and

arms of the men at the controls—forward, reverse, turn—pushing the
dirt with the powerful blade of the bulldozer and sending the mound
of rock and dirt over the cliff—dropping the blade into the ground at
the precise moment to prevent the bulldozer from going over the edge.
Reverse, turn, and back again against the mountain for another bite.
The smaller D-7s would shift the dirt on the road and then graders
and rollers would pack the dirt. Sometimes small rock crushers were
used to turn the stones into gravel. More often the soldiers would use
jack-hammers to break down the rock, and large gangs of local Naga
tribesmen used small hammers to further break the stones down to
gravel for the roadbed.

The D-8 bulldozer operators took special pride in their sometimes
dangerous but fulfilling work. Most of these men learned to operate
heavy equipment in the army; they would not have been hired to do
that kind of work back home because of job discrimination. But in
the army, they were tech sergeants (five stripes) and master sergeants
(six stripes).

Our outfit moved up the road two more times, in twenty-mile moves.
There were now about eight battalions working on the road, and each
was given a stretch to maintain. The road was in constant need of
repair and improvement because of the heavy traffic of truck convoys
bringing supplies to the troops fighting the Japanese up ahead, and
the heavy rains of the monsoon season, which caused road cave-ins
and rock slides.

Things settled down after a few months and most of the work was
confined to daylight hours, except in emergencies.

Merrill's Marauders and the Mars Task Force were two of the
fighting American units that passed us on foot with their pack mules
on their way to engage the Japanese on the front. They were seasoned
jungle fighters who had been brought up from the Pacific islands
campaign. An infantry regiment of French West African soldiers also
passed us.

Small world, I met my high school buddy Lloyd Edwards, by chance. He was one of the five black guys who graduated from Automotive High School with me and got a job with the bus company in the paint shop. He was drafted and was driving a truck in the quartermaster corps on the Ledo Road.

In north Burma it could be oppressively hot during the day, but in the hills and mountains it was relatively cool at night. Every man slept with a mosquito bar over his bed, and he would face a court martial if he didn't. Malaria was a serious problem in the area, and there were pills put into our drinking water that gave a yellowish color to light-skinned people. As things settled down they would show movies in the company, and we saw movie stars like Alice Faye, Fred Astaire, and Dorothy Lamour.

Around payday every month, big crap games in the tents at night moved lots of money and left some guys broke and others happy. Among the small group of inveterate gamblers in the outfit, the most colorful was a guy named Sugarstick, from Detroit. The stakes got higher and higher as the money changed hands, until one guy ended up with most of the available money. Some guys played poker and a card game popular among blacks called "Tonque." Some guys wrote letters home sitting on their bunks and reminiscing.

I worked in the motor pool and didn't like it at all. I had the same Uncle Tom sergeant I had had at Myrtle Beach, and I soon found myself transferred out of the motor pool onto the rock gang breaking down stones on the road with a pneumatic drill. One day, while I was taking a break from the drill, the company commander Captain Nichols drove up. I continued resting (which I later reasoned was stupid and immature). As punishment I was put on K.P. duty in the kitchen.

The kitchen fed the company of about 150 men three meals a day. The kitchen worked two shifts of six men each under the mess sergeant. Each of the two shifts worked every other day. On your day on, you were up at 3:00 AM to prepare and serve breakfast. Then you cleaned up and prepared lunch and then dinner. After the dinner clean-up you were free. The next morning the other crew took over, and did the same thing. Our crew had that whole next day off until 3 AM the next morning. I fitted in OK as a cook's helper. I was a pretty good amateur cook from my Boy Scout days and from watching around the house. And, truthfully, a fair part of overseas cooking was opening cans.

It was getting toward December and in my new spare time I made up a few Christmas cards to send home. Some of the men saw them and pretty soon I had a little business going. I would design a card, trace it over on carbon paper and then add color. I was pretty good at drawing in school and it became a hobby. I would charge a couple of dollars for a card, and although the process was slow, I did a nice business. And it kept me occupied in my spare time.

By the time our company made its second major move, things began to settle down considerably. Merrill's Marauders and our allies were slowly pushing the enemy farther and farther back, and the Ledo Road was getting closer and closer to its link up with the old Burma Road. Our battalion was maintaining its stretch of the road, but it was a constant battle against the monsoon rains and the incessant rumble of the truck convoys as they made their way to the front.

The five other guys in my kitchen crew were fairly easygoing and friendly. We lived in the same tent. One of them, whom everybody called Bimbo, took care of the garbage and generally kept the kitchen clean. He was a short, roly-poly sort of guy who seemed a bit older than the rest of us. As a matter of fact we often got his dander up by accusing him of putting his age lower than it really was to get into the army. Bimbo lived in Harlem and, despite his demeanor, he was quite informed in many ways. He had read books like Victor Hugo's *Les Miserables*, and was a gifted conversationalist. He had a marvelous wit and a keen sense of humor, and came off as a sort of hobo-intellectual. I enjoyed talking with Bimbo, and we played a riotous game of checkers, which we were both good at.

Another Brooklyn guy in our tent named Jimmy Huston was in charge of keeping the company supplied with safe drinking water. He was a good alto sax player and knew music theory. Soon I was learning intervals, triads, and chords, major, minor, sharps and flats. But that was just the start. I was approaching my twentieth birthday, and things started falling in place, things that just seemed to open up my head.

While I was working on music theory, our company built a little chapel and started a small choir of about seven or eight guys, and I was invited to be a member. They told me I had a promising voice and encouraged me to practice a couple of solos.

Around the same time, they had gotten a new field organ, and they gave me the old one. I patched it up and took it to my tent and learned to play a few chords, which helped me in my theory lessons. And I had plenty of time to study and learn. After all, here I was stuck in the jungle of north Burma with nowhere to go at night and working in the kitchen only every other day. I'm not saying I never played cards or shot crap or bull-shitted with the guys. But this whole study and learning process was something new to me and I was eating it up. The vocational high school I went to never really required homework. So the whole idea of studying anything was brand new to me. But now I was driving myself, and it was strangely exhilarating.

For a while, this education process focused only on music. Then I discovered that Captain Smith, the chaplain and only black officer in our battalion, had been a high school German language teacher in Mississippi. When he got the idea that I was eager to learn just about everything, he sort of took me under his wing. So I started to study German with him.

At the time, it didn't seem strange, but when I think back, it was kind of odd: a black high school offering German, and its teacher stuck here on the fringe of India where they spoke mostly Hindustani.

I also took on the reading of books, anything I could get my hands on: history, philosophy, religion, English literature. Even though I worked one long day and was off the next, I got in some study time on my workdays too. I carried slips of paper in each pocket with things to memorize and practice in between meal breaks or any other free time.

Oyama Tate, a guy about 25 from Iowa, was an assistant organist in his church back home. He played the field organ and directed our little choir. Leon Hepburn from New York was also an experienced choir singer. I had never sung in a group before. I began to develop my voice, and I sang a solo in the chapel about every two weeks. I was gaining confidence and developing my singing with encouragement from some of the others. And I enjoyed doing it all.

My theory studies with Jimmy Huston were helping me learn to sight-read music and learn musical values. Our outfit got an alto sax from Special Services, and Jimmy gave me saxophone lessons for about four months, long enough to play a little.

Chaplain Smith, the high school German language teacher in Mississippi, was supplying me with various types of books to read. He also gave me some pamphlets and material on black history, a subject which was not generally known to blacks prior to World War II, especially those in the inner city ghettos of the north. I had heard of Frederick Douglas and Harriett Tubman, but knew hardly anything about them. I had heard of Marcus Garvey through my mother. There was no mention of black people in any of the books I had in grammar or high school. There were no black role models for black children to emulate. They knew little beyond the fact that their ancestors were slaves and had been brought to America in bondage and freed by Abraham Lincoln in the Civil War. As a result, most black children had difficulty relating beyond their grandparents on their family tree. They did not know of the exploits of black people like Jean Baptiste du

Sable (1745-1818), a black Haitian fur trapper who founded the city of Chicago; Ira Aldridge, the great Shakespearean actor in England (1807-1869); Joseph Cinque, who led the mutiny on the slave ship "Amistad"; Robert Smalls, who daringly stole a confederate gunboat and delivered it to the Union Army during the Civil War; Nat Turner, who led a slave rebellion in Virginia in 1831; Matthew Henson who discovered the North Pole with Admiral Peary on April 6, 1909.

These icons of black history were unknown to the vast number of blacks until after World War II (1945). The projection of black history after 1945 and throughout the Civil Rights movement did much to strengthen the resolve of blacks in their struggle for equality, and especially served as icons to black youth. Based on the information that I was absorbing about the black condition from Chaplain Smith, I began to put together my own scenario regarding my family. It went like this:

It was a long time ago, I don't know exactly when—I'm sure nobody does: it could have been as far back as 1790, or 1690, or even 1590. But somewhere back there in time, at least one of my mother's ancestors was captured, bound and shackled and put on a boat at one of those West African ports—Dahomey, Gold Coast, Senegal, Camaroon, Nigeria—one of those places—and the boat sailed for the New World. That made them children of the Middle Passage, as the crossing of the Atlantic Ocean by slave traders was called. Along this torturous voyage, some died of sickness, some committed suicide, and after the slave trade was declared illegal, some boat loads of slaves were flung into the sea by the crews of the illegal slavers to escape detection when a patrol ship approached. Arriving in the so-called New World at a slave trading station—perhaps Jamaica, Cuba or Barbados—these Africans were sold on auction blocks to the highest bidder.

Generations later, in the year 1917, my mother at the age of 23, daughter of a free woman (slavery had been abolished in the English-speaking Caribbean in 1838), granddaughter of an ex-slave, left the shore of Barbados and sailed for North America—the United States of America, the land of opportunity—and settled in Brooklyn, New York.

Way back there in that stretch of time—could have been 1790, or 1690, or even 1590—much the same thing happened to my father's ancestors. They were also survivors of the crossing. Only, that boat veered more to the north and landed at Virginia or South Carolina or Maryland. Whichever way, his ancestors were also sold on the auction block to the highest bidder. Cotton was the crop that brought the slave trade to North America. Millions of Africans were brought in bondage to the southern states as good, cheap labor to grow and harvest cotton to supply the mills of Boston and Manchester, which helped to nurture the Industrial Revolution. Several generations later, I don't know exactly how many, my father—in 1918, grandson of a slave and son of a free woman—hopped a freight train in Virginia headed for New York in hopes of a war job, and he too settled in Brooklyn.

The Allies were now taking the offensive, chasing Rommel out of North Africa and invading Sicily and Italy. We were all waiting for what was called the Second Front in Europe, the invasion that was going to defeat Hitler and the Nazis. Meanwhile the Russians were turning back the German invasion at the Battle of Stalingrad.

My German language and music theory studies, plus all the reading I was trying to do, pretty much filled all my free time and then some. But I was getting into it all. I'll tell you how good I was getting: One day we—three members of the choir—were walking down the road, and we started to sing the "Hallelujah Chorus" from Handel's *Messiah* in three-part harmony from beginning to end, without any accompaniment. We thought that we were pretty damn good. And maybe we were.

I didn't know it then, but I had started a singing career. That's because I was getting over my initial stage fright and really looking forward to singing a solo at the Sunday morning chapel service. I was being coached to sing the classical repertoire where you learn to project your voice, rather than the pop songs where you sing into a microphone. I was also becoming acquainted with some of the works of the great composers, such as Franz Schubert, Johannes Brahms and Richard Wagner, many of whose melodies were used in hymnals and concert songs.

At the time Marian Anderson, a contralto, was the foremost black singer on the concert stage and Roland Hayes, a tenor, was the only black male of national concert stage status. Todd Duncan, a baritone, was seen on Broadway starring in such black productions as *Show Boat* and *Porgy and Bess*. Paul Robeson, the All-American football player from Rutgers, actor and movie personality, was renowned for his deep bass singing and speaking voice. I had grown up memorizing all the pop songs on the radio, and now I was learning to sing many of the songs in the concert repertoire. By the age of 20 I began to envision myself as a future star of the concert stage. Seriously.

Being on the Ledo Road in Assam on the Indian border with Burma, you seldom saw anyone but other soldiers except for a few Naga tribesmen, and often the day-to-day life could be humdrum. In our outfit there were occasional incidents to break the monotony—some comic, others horrifying, especially because we hadn't seen any combat in our assignments. Like when Sergeant Cook, the company mailman, who traveled armed with a pistol, was brandishing his gun and foolishly playing around with another soldier. The soldier, frightened, grabbed his arm, and in the scuffle, Sergeant Cook was shot with his own gun. He lay there on the ground bleeding from a bullet hole in his stomach. He was mumbling about his wife and child back home in the States, while the men gathered around and tried to get him to medical aid by putting him in a truck, but he died en route.

If there was anything we knew for sure it was that guns weren't for fooling around. Even so, a while later two guys in B Company got into an argument and one ran for his M1 rifle. The other ran behind a tree and the first one shot right through that tree, killing him on the spot.

One morning a soldier ran by me as I was coming out of my tent. He was on fire. He had been down by the motor pool washing his truck with a mixture of gasoline. He then went to his tent and was putting a piece of wood in the stove, and the gas fumes on his clothes caught fire. He ran a few more steps, and fell. The soldier died from the burns. (At first, some of my tent mates had thought it was me.)

"Blowtop" was the nickname of the cook on the other shift. One day he was making a bread pudding for dinner made of old pieces of bread from previous meals. The old bread was kept in a large rectangular baking pan. "Blowtop" mixed the old bread with evaporated milk, sugar, vanilla, and the other ingredients that the pudding called for and put it in the stove to bake.

At dinner time the men passed in front of the counter and we put the meal on their mess kits. Pretty soon someone came back to the counter and claimed he saw a small bone in the bread pudding. Someone else came back also and, upon examination, it was discovered that a rat had been cooked in the bread pudding. The word quickly spread and some men began vomiting. Some of the guys got very angry and were ready to fight. Needless to say, the kitchen crew carried a low profile the rest of the evening, and the mess sergeant stayed out of sight all the next day.

Then a soldier in B Company whom everybody feared because of his volatile temper, got into a scuffle and then went up the road. Lieut. Cadie from our company approached him and demanded that the soldier surrender his gun. The soldier refused, and Lieut. Cadie walked right up to disarm him. The soldier fired, and Lieut. Cadie fell dead.

Our company was alerted and a posse was organized to hunt the soldier in the surrounding hills, but we couldn't find him. So the military police were put on the case. A few months later he was discovered living in a remote tribal community. The soldier had married the chief's daughter. He was taken to the stockade in Ledo to await a trial. Somehow he escaped and was at large for about a month before they captured him again. After a quick trial, he was hanged in Ledo. Along with the Wednesday night movie that was also outdoors, these were among the memorable events in camp besides road building and equipment maintenance.

As the Ledo Road reached farther into north Burma, we moved our base three times to keep up with our progress. After a year and a half, our battalion got two-week furloughs for R and R (rest and recreation). We piled onto the train for Calcutta. We had had enough of the jungle heat and the hills and bush of Burma. We were ready for the big city.

And Calcutta was the big city, teeming with people. In those days, India was still a colony of the British Empire and there were lots of troops from Britain, Burma, Ceylon, and the rest of their empire. There were many restaurants, especially Chinese. The R and R troops were quartered in a comfortable camp. In town, there was a big U.S.O. center where many of the guys congregated and where some local girls came to help entertain and dance with the service men. The streets carried a fair share of beggars, con men, and hashish peddlers. Of course, in a big city like Calcutta the main attraction for many service men were the numerous bordellos in certain districts. The soldiers stationed in Calcutta seemed to be hostile to the soldiers coming in out of the hills and jungles because we generally had much more money to spend, having been holed up for more than a year with nowhere to spend even our meager GI pay.

Shortly after we got back to camp, we heard the news of the German surrender and the end of the war in Europe. But not much changed for us. I went back into the kitchen routine and my studies. The entire war was now centered on Southeast Asia and the Pacific as we began preparation for the invasion of Japan. We were already in that part of the world, but that summer, the armed forces in Europe were looking at the grim prospects of landings in Japan that would be worse than what happened at the beaches of Normandy on D Day.

And then it was over. An American plane dropped an atom bomb on Hiroshima. Then, before we knew what an atom bomb was, the air force dropped another one on the city of Nagasaki. Two bombs killed hundreds of thousands of people, and two cities disappeared. And the Japanese surrendered unconditionally. V-J Day was celebrated throughout the world, and we were going home. Later we might think about the awesome new power that humbled Japan so quickly. But all that mattered then was we were going home.

While we waited to be rotated home, we kept working on our section of the road. But we weren't at war anymore, and we all began thinking about home. I had never even thought about going back to school in the past, because I had graduated from a vocational high school, and I figured that was the end of the line for education. But once I got involved with studying music and languages and all that reading, I started thinking that I was going to go to college. And the government was going to pay my way. The GI Bill of Rights, among other things, would allow any GI to go to any school or college that would accept him. The government would pay your tuition and books and give you $75 a month for room and board, for 12 months plus a month for every month you served.

So I spent the next two months studying and practicing harder than ever. My life was going to change in a big way.

Our rotation came up the end of October, and we finally boarded the ship for home. It had taken us 34 days from New York to Bombay, but on the return trip we went through the Suez Canal and the Mediterranean and the trip took just ten days, with no zigzagging to evade submarines. We arrived at Camp Kilmer, New Jersey, and I was mustered out of the army as a private first class one week later, November 30, 1945, to be exact.

Although blacks were in segregated units, usually commanded by white officers, they did gain experience leading men, as sergeants, master sergeants, and first sergeants, and in some outfits, as officers. Before the war, civilian employers seldom, if ever, allowed blacks to move up to positions of authority. A. Philip Randolph, the head of the black Brotherhood of Sleeping Car Porters and a leading labor leader, convinced President Roosevelt to establish the Fair Employment Practices Commission, which led the way to equal opportunity employment in the federal government and the defense industry. Randolph also formed the League for Non-violent Civil Disobedience in the armed forces. Under pressure from Randolph and the league, President Truman issued an executive order that began the process of ending segregation in the military.

Col. William J. Green, who had been chief road engineer of the Ledo Road, championed the work of the black soldiers who built it. He was called to Washington by President Harry Truman to sit on the commission that in 1947 began to integrate the armed forces of the United States. That would become one of the many actions that eventually led to what became known as the civil rights movement in America.

At times life in the army was an ordeal, but bitching about it was the normal posture for every soldier. And I bitched my share, I guess. But for me, going in at 18 and coming out three years later, still a very young man, with the experience of travel, of mingling with soldiers and people from different walks of life, taking full advantage of my forced leisure time, and now the prospect of a higher education, I felt that my experience was decidedly positive. Of course, I kept these sentiments to myself, as the "proper" attitude of most soldiers was to consider their time in the army a "terrible sacrifice."

# SOLFA 5

*sol*

BROOKLYN, LIKE EVERYTHING else in my life, had changed a lot over the three years. The black population of Brooklyn had probably doubled, and many people settled there from Latin America, Asia, and lots of parts of Europe. I looked up a couple of my old buddies, and we compared experiences.

Somehow, the Albany Avenue gang that I used to hang out with had lost its appeal. In the old days we went to the movies, spent Sunday evenings at the Savoy Ballroom in Harlem, St. Peter Claver's Friday night basketball games and dances, or went over to Dave's and Mike's house, dancing, playing cards, or just sitting around bull-shitting. Guys got jobs and girlfriends. We had grown up. Some guys even went back to school, but none in my group as far as I knew. Also, the girl I liked on Albany Avenue had married a soldier.

A couple of months out of the army I was back on my old job as an apprentice mechanic at the Fifth Avenue Coach Co. (veterans had priority for their old jobs). I enrolled in the spring semester at Brooklyn College at night and was studying Italian grammar and music harmony, because I was hoping to take the entrance exam and get accepted at the Juilliard School of Music.

Here's how I got pointed to that school: When I came out of the army, my brother Will, by then 17, was working part-time for the boys' department of New York City Mission Society and Camp Minisink, and his mentor was a black carpenter-contractor named Herb Von King. He was a prominent figure in Brooklyn youth work and was the scoutmaster of Troop 219 at Fleet Street Baptist Church and one of the organizers of the Minisink cadet corps. The corps began as a winter activity of the staff and campers of Camp Minisink (near Port Jervis in southwestern New York state), run by the New York City Mission Society. Herb was my brother's mentor from age 12 in the scout and camping program. (Tomkins Park in Brooklyn was renamed Herbert Von King Park when he died.)

During his Boy Scout days, Will became interested in American Indian lore and dances and organized a group of dancers in the troop who performed at scout events around the city. As a teenager he was also interested in developing his voice and became a student in the preparatory department of the Juilliard School of Music. (Years later Juilliard moved down to Lincoln Center, closed its prep school, added drama and other programs and dropped "of Music" from its name.)

Will was attending school at Juilliard when I was discharged from the army. When I told him about my own interest in music he introduced me to his teacher, Paul Kruger, who agreed to give me voice lessons privately. I started with the standard Italian repertory mixed with some English ballads.

So there I was, working my bus mechanic job from 8:00 AM to 4:30PM, five days a week, after a subway ride of an hour and a 15-minute walk; attending Brooklyn College two nights a week; taking one private voice lesson a week; practicing daily vocal exercises and learning songs. All that left no time for anything else, but it was worth it.

After my one-year apprenticeship at the bus company before the war, they had put me on a five-man gang that worked on overhauling bus chassis. We had to wear bandanas over our noses and mouths. This dirt, coupled with occasional gas fumes from the buses, gave me second thoughts about working in such environments, as a voice student. The floor bosses probably didn't like the idea of my going to school, especially for something as distant from labor as music.

I decided to work until mid-May—the time of my final exams at Brooklyn College—take my two weeks vacation and quit the job. In the meantime, I was getting set to apply to Juilliard, and with the $75 a month the GI Bill would pay plus the $1,000 I had saved in the army, a lot of money in those days, I felt I could get by.

I had moved back home when I got out of the army. My father and my mother had been separated since the war started. We were a poor working-class family, but we did not live beyond our means. We were able to keep things moving along. My mother was a great manager and provider and could still put together a tasty meal. My brother and I were able to take care of ourselves. My father had been working as a building janitor and slept at the job. My mother had been working in a uniform factory as a seamstress.

Meanwhile, I joined St. Phillips Church. I had been christened and sometimes attended Sunday school there. As I have said, my scout troop was there too. It was my mother's denomination back home. Barbadians were British subjects, and the Episcopal Church is the Church of England. I joined the church and the choir because I felt it was in harmony with my studies, mood and state of mind at the time. With about 40 people, the church choir was solemn and imposing in black and white robes marching down the center aisle to the choir stalls. St. Phillips was at the time the leading black Episcopal Church in Brooklyn. The common joke was that your daughter was not really married if the ceremony did not take place at St. Phillips. Being an Episcopal church, it had a large number of members of West Indian descent.

Friday evening was choir practice. The choir was a volunteer group, many of whose members had been there for years. Mostly they didn't read music, but learned by rote or ear, as is the case with most non-professional choirs. The choirmaster, E. Aldama Jackson A.G.O. (American Guild of Organists) taught piano, organ, and voice at his home studio. The soloists were usually his private students, and they were not brilliant voices by any definition. But Jackson was fearless in the face of the masters. He would tackle just about anything. Handel's *Messiah*, Gounod's *Seven Last Words*, Haydn's *Creation*, Rossini's *Stabat Mater*, Bach's *Christmas Oratorio*, and Mendelssohn's *Elijah* were regularly heard during the course of the year, complete or in excerpts. At times, the situation would become desperate, but in the end we finished. However, going over such a wealth of material was great practice for me in sight-reading and familiarized me with the great oratorios of these masters. I also developed a camaraderie with a few of the young choir members.

I was accepted at Juilliard and I took the same A train that I used to take to work at the bus company on 125th Street; I still walked to Broadway, but turned left, rather than right, to go to 122nd Street. Juilliard was a very well known music school that enjoyed enormous prestige in musical circles. Its students came from everywhere and were generally musically precocious. They were of college age and beyond and there was also a preparatory department for high school students. The theory and music lessons that I had practiced so diligently overseas, served me well in passing the entrance exam. Also colleges and universities bent a little to accept veterans, because they knew that the U.S. government guaranteed the tuition fees.

The school was located right off Riverside Park and the Hudson River in a sprawling academic community that included Columbia University, Barnard College, Union Theological Seminary, the Jewish

Theological Seminary, Grant's Tomb, the International House and Riverside Church (built by the Rockefeller family). It was an area highly conducive to meditation, thought and study. I often sat in Riverside Park or in the cool pews of Riverside Church on a hot summer afternoon.

Lucius Metz was my voice teacher. We continued with the Italian repertoire and some English ballads. I took classes in sight-singing and music dictation and chorus under the direction of Peter Wilhousky, who was then conductor of the All City High School Chorus. I developed a few friends in the student body.

I met Ella Mae Bowman, who was only 20 but had just graduated from Brooklyn College with a degree in French. She was a piano major at Juilliard and taught piano at the studio apartment in Brooklyn where she lived with her mother. She was active in her church and taught Sunday school there. She helped me a lot as an accompanist and we became friends.

Starting in summer school and continuing through the academic year, I listened to a wide range of symphonic music at the Juilliard record library: Beethoven's "Fifth Symphony," Grieg's "Peer Gynt Suite," Tchaikovsky's "Romeo and Juliet," Schubert's "Unfinished," Rachmaninoff's "Second Piano Concerto," among others. I also attended some of the New York Philharmonic summer concerts high up in the cheap seats at Lewisohn Stadium on the nearby campus of City College.

The political climate was rapidly changing in America at the end of World War II. Many people, especially the youth, were anxious for change. With what seemed to be a new society in the making, college campuses took on a serious and somber mood, fueled by the presence of many veterans on campus. Blacks began to form their own political clubs especially in the "inner cities," and some became district leaders in their constituencies. The first black to be elected to public office in

New York State was Hulan Jack (born in British Guiana) who served first in the state legislature from Harlem starting in 1941 and later as borough president. The first black elected in Brooklyn was Bertram Baker (born in Nevis, West Indies) representing the Bedford-Stuyvesant area in 1949.

After a busy and happy time at summer school, I went to Washington, D.C., to visit my sister. The tensions released by the first attempts at integration after the war created many and varied responses. My sister had been recruited right out of high school in 1941 to join the government work force in Washington and started as a clerk-typist. While there she met and married Clarzell Jenkins who also worked for the government following his medical discharge from the Navy.

One night Clarzell (a light-brown man of about 250 pounds) and I stopped off at the local deli a couple of blocks from their apartment to buy some groceries. We entered the store just ahead of two elderly white women. At the counter, the clerk looked past Clarzell and asked the two women what they wanted. Clarzell took this as a racial insult and told the man that he had come first. The man glared at Clarzell, leaned across the counter in Clarzell's face, and said, "And suppose I don't want to serve you?!" Clarzell's eyes narrowed and the next move was his hand landing against the counterman's jaw with a sound like a firecracker. The whole print of his hand was on the man's face. One old lady let out a shriek. The counterman remained frozen on the spot. Clarzell stood there in his tracks, eye to eye with the counterman. In about four seconds that seemed like an eternity, I made the first move. I grabbed Clarzell's arm and said, "Let's go!" As we walked toward the door I could almost feel a bullet in my back. Clarzell muttered, "My money's just as good as anybody else's." As we turned from the door, Clarzell said, "Don't run." I was extremely nervous and my heart was in my mouth until we turned the corner.

Later that evening I thought about the ordeal, and how close to death we could have been. I felt so anxious for my sister there in her little apartment with a two-year-old son. How could a casual trip to a deli take such a dangerous turn? If the coin had flipped the other way, she could have been without husband and brother—all in a half-hour. All the frustrations, anxieties, and ignorance were now building more and more as the country came to grips with racial discrimination.

I never mentioned the incident to my sister, and I never discussed it with Clarzell. I had mixed feelings about him being so stupid as to put his future and his family's in jeopardy—for such a paltry reward. But I had to secretly admire his manhood on its own terms. He had had enough and expressed that. Dangerous certainly but admirable too. After all, isn't that what America is all about?

From Washington, D.C., I went to visit Bill Reliford, an army buddy in Detroit. He had previously introduced me to his sister, Geneva, in Brooklyn where she was a design student at Pratt Institute. She lived at the "colored" YWCA residence on Ashford Place, a converted brownstone not far from Pratt. We dated once in a while.

That fall I started Juilliard in the extension program with classes mostly in the evening. Paul Kruger, my voice teacher, and I continued with the Italian anthology and then got into German lieder. Songs from Schubert's song cycles "Die Schöne Müllerin" and "Winterreise" and the Schumann "Dichterliebe" kept me busy. I was now singing art songs in Italian, German and French, besides English. All along, I had made a special study of Negro Spirituals as compiled and arranged by such renowned black musicians as John W. Work, Hall Johnson and Harry T. Burleigh. Most black concert singers were expected to close their program with a set of spirituals—which to me at the time was a plus. I took a course in music theory, more sight-singing and dictation, French phonetics and a piano minor.

It was fairly evident that many of the students at Juilliard had a sense of mission and were accustomed to long hours of practice and drills on their instruments. The singers saw themselves as tomorrow's concert artists—traveling the world in the echoes of Enrico Caruso, Jussi Björling, Maria Callas or Lili Pons—or as stars of the theatre or film.

There was a sprinkling of black students who were probably drawn to the field of classical music by the success of such concert singers as Roland Hayes, Todd Duncan, Marian Anderson and Camilla Williams despite color bars. In many cases, the black students' participation in their church choirs and Sunday afternoon musicals was useful for preparing to enter the field of musical performance, both classical and popular. There was an underlying feeling that music was one of the few fields that blacks would be accepted in, talent counted even more than color, up to a point.

I started going regularly to concerts at Carnegie Hall, Town Hall and Times Hall among other places to hear various types of music performed by such stars as Kirsten Flagstad, Mack Harrell, Ferruccio Tagliavini, Dorothy Maynor, Roland Hayes, Richard Tauber and Jussi Björling. I sat in the cheap seats, of course. I went a few times to the Salmaggi Opera Co. in downtown Brooklyn where I saw Italian opera at low prices and, although the productions were second rate—sometimes to the point of being comic—they were lively and informative. There were also a lot of student concerts and seminars at Juilliard worth attending. I even went to the Met a couple of times.

Among the friends I made at Juilliard, about a dozen of us black students formed a group called the Alpha Mu Sigma Society. We met monthly at the apartments of students who lived with their families in Harlem or the Bronx. Andy Frierson, who later sang with the New York City Opera Company, Virginia Capers, who later starred in the musical *Raisin*; Olga James, who played opposite Sammy Davis in *Mr. Wonderful*; Elma Alexander, the pianist, and Elayne Jones, who later became the tympanist for the American Symphony Orchestra, were among the members.

For student singers and performers, there were numerous opportunities at local concerts, meetings, dinners, church services and Sunday afternoon socials in auditoriums and private homes. They provided useful experience developing rapport with audiences and overcoming stage fright.

As a result of the war effort, which created a shortage of manpower, blacks had been integrated into the workforce. There was much more mixing of the races than ever before. Blacks moved in large numbers from the farms and plantations of the south, seeking jobs in the factories of the north. The Mississippi Delta blacks went north to Chicago and Detroit, and the Atlantic Coast blacks settled in Newark, Washington, D.C., and New York. Blacks also came from the Caribbean islands. Blacks were going to high school and even college in increasing numbers, and as a result of our participation in the war effort and our service in the armed forces, we began asking for a larger share of the pie. This met with much opposition in some parts of the country—especially the South.

Black leaders, such as Adam Clayton Powell Jr, began to emerge in the black ghettos of New York, Chicago, Detroit and Los Angeles, with an assist from the white progressives in the labor movement and especially progressive Jews and Marxists. The American Communist Party made a particular bid for the black vote, even running a black candidate for vice-president. Black universities and even the black churches began to assume a grass roots militancy and adopt a political agenda that was not as evident in the past. During this time there were growing signs of a radical change in race relations and civil rights in America.

There also existed a sort of affinity between many blacks and progressive Jews rooted in a common history of discrimination and persecution. Blacks saw in their condition a similarity with the Jews of the Old Testament who were enslaved by the Pharaohs of Egypt and centuries later banished from Spain by the Inquisition, and who had been ghettoized in most of the countries of Europe over the centuries. The Jewish odyssey is passionately reflected in black spirituals with titles such as "Go Down, Moses," "Little David, Play on Your Harp," "Ezekiel Saw the Wheel", and "Turn Back Pharaoh's Army." Part of the attraction of the "white man's religion" to slaves was the promise of deliverance from bondage as depicted in the the Old Testament. The Negro spiritual says:

> Didn't My Lord Deliver Daniel?
> He delivered Daniel from the lion's den
> An' Jonah from the belly of the whale
> An' the Hebrew children from the fiery furnace
> An' why not every man!

From my early days of serious study, which started in the army in India and Burma, I began, with the help of Chaplain Smith, to delve into English literature. In my spare time, I read a bit of history, religion, politics, philosophy and ethics, along with learning songs and music. I also learned by heart some of the more popular dramatic soliloquies and poems. I continued this practice throughout my college years. Although I had been a rather gregarious, sometimes even loud, person, I now sought out and relished the solitary peaceful moments, dealing with my thoughts. Almost without realizing it, I began to savor the words that I had memorized, not precisely owning those of others, but beginning somewhere deep to feel a need to create my own.

At times when I was walking alone along the Ledo Road in north Burma, I would declaim:

> Friends, Romans, countrymen, lend me your ears:
> I come to bury Caesar, not to praise him.
> The evil that men do lives after them;
> The good is oft interred with their bones . . . .
>                                        William Shakespeare

Or on the trail in the foothills of the Green Mountains of New Hampshire, on my days off from counseling at Camp Rabbit Hollow:

> Had I the heaven's embroidered cloths,
> Enwrought with golden and silver light,
> The blue and the dim and the dark cloths
> Of night and light and the half-light,
>
> I would spread the cloths under your feet:
> But I, being poor, have only my dreams . . . .
>> William Butler Yeats

Perhaps along the shore of Lake Michigan in downtown Chicago:

> "The fog creeps in on little cat feet . . . ."
>> Carl Sandburg

On my day off from counseling at Camp Minisink at High Point Park, NY:

> To be or not to be: that is the question:
> Whether 'tis nobler in the mind to suffer
> The slings and arrows of outrageous fortune,
> Or to take arms against a sea of troubles,
> And thus opposing, end them . . .
>> William Shakespeare

In the woods outside Red Bank, NJ:

> Yea, though' I walk through the valley of the shadow of
>   death,

> I will fear no evil . . . Surely goodness and mercy shall
>     follow me all the days of my life . . .
>
>                              23<sup>rd</sup> Psalm

On a stroll around the Coliseum at the University of Southern
California:

> Up, you mighty race! You can accomplish what you
> will!
> Black is Beautiful!
>
>                              Marcus Garvey

Or just sitting in my room romanticizing:

> Go, lovely Rose
> Tell her that wastes her time and me,
> That tho' she knows,
> When I resemble her to thee,
> How sweet and fair she seems to be.
> . . . . . . . . . .
> Small is the worth
> Of beauty from the light retired:
> Bid her come forth,
> Suffer herself to be desired.
> . . . . . . . . . .
> Then die—that she
> The common fate of all things rare
> May read in thee;
> How small a part of time they share
> That are so wondrous sweet and fair!
>
>                              Edmund Waller

As the evening sun falls, golden red, on the edge of the desert outside Tucson, Arizona:

> FOUR SCORE AND SEVEN YEARS AGO, OUR FATHERS BROUGHT FORTH UPON THIS CONTINENT A NEW NATION CONCEIVED IN LIBERTY AND DEDICATED TO THE PROPOSITION THAT ALL MEN ARE CREATED EQUAL . . .
>
> Abraham Lincoln

At the end of my first year at Juilliard I was pretty stretched out from studies, but I had a feeling of accomplishment. I had applied myself and had learned so much about so many things both in and out of the classroom. Geneva Jones told me about her aunt in Red Bank, New Jersey, who knew of a senior citizen retreat that was run by a relative on the outskirts of town and would rent me a room quite cheap where I could relax and unwind for a couple of weeks. I arrived in Red Bank and was directed to the retreat. It was in a quiet wooded area. There were senior citizen guests on the other side of the building I never saw. In my simple but comfortable room I was completely alone with my books and papers from which I was memorizing songs, doing theory exercise, language study, or general reading. They prepared meals for me, and sometimes I would carry a lunch on my walks. I was quite content.

After two weeks I returned to New York and spent the balance of the summer going to a few summer concerts, looking up a few friends and family and getting set for the next semester.

The second year at Juilliard was pretty much more of the same, with Mom working part-time and my brother engrossed in his youth leadership job with the New York City Mission Society, and his work with the Boy Scouts of America. I also took a class in theatre at the neighboring Brander Matthews Theater of Columbia University. About this time I met a new member of the St. Phillips choir named Joe Purviance. We would get together at times and discuss various aspects of the theater as well as acting techniques. Purviance was a graduate student at NYU, majoring in theater. He had got a bachelor's degree at a black college in Maryland. Then he got a grant from the state of Maryland to study outside the state for his master's. Under federal law at that time (upheld by the US Supreme Court in Plessey v. Ferguson in 1896) "separate but equal" permitted segregated education. But the segregating states had to comply by paying the way for many black students seeking higher degrees out of state, because they could not attend white segregated schools of higher learning in their own states.

Purviance also acquainted me with the American Negro Theatre in New York, which began under the leadership of Abram Hill and Frederick O'Neal in the mid-1940s. They were beginning to receive wide recognition with the production of *Anna Lucasta* and became the spawning ground for black actors such as Hilda Simms, Canada Lee, Earl Hyman, Rosetta LeNoire, Sidney Poitier, Ossie Davis, and Ruby Dee.

During my second year I even had the audacity to present myself in a concert at the local YMCA on Bedford Avenue in Brooklyn. It was a program of the art songs I had studied, closing with a set of spirituals. I considered myself quite enterprising and enticed my friends, relatives, and a few choir members to buy tickets. Ella Bowman was my accompanist and also played a couple of piano solos on the program. In my vocal studies my songs were in the high baritone range, although my teacher felt that my true range was tenor, and with more training my voice would ensue the higher register.

Meanwhile I developed a condition that was giving me frequent colds and tonsillitis and affecting my voice. At the clinic I went to, it was diagnosed as a deviation of the septum, which caused a post-nasal drip. The doctor and my voice teacher agreed that I should have my tonsils removed, and I did. But the condition persisted and continued to hamper my vocal studies. At the end of my second year at Juilliard I decided to spend the next year in the Southwest where the dry climate was better for respiratory problems like mine. I chose the University of Arizona in Tucson.

It was going to be Arizona in the fall, but the summer of 1948 was going to be closer to home. I was asked to be a summer camp counselor. James H. Robinson, minister of the Church of the Master in Harlem, operated twin camps—Forest Lake for girls and Rabbit Hollow for boys—in Winchester, New Hampshire. These camps were interracial but served mostly poor black kids from New York City. Robinson was a dynamic and influential leader in New York, as well as a Chubb Fellow at Yale. He was a guest speaker at many institutions and was in the front rank of interracial affairs. He recruited most of his counselors from Ivy League colleges as well as some black colleges, and he assembled a formidable group of bright, energetic students as his counselors. A few years later, he would start Operation Crossroads Africa, which sent hundreds of students to Africa on work projects. The Peace Corps was developed by the United States government and was patented after Operation Crossroads Africa. Robinson was truly a man with a silver tongue, and a tireless worker who would sometimes, for emphasis, join the detail cleaning out the camp latrines.

I was a natural as a camp counselor. I had been a boy scout in Brooklyn and was good at hiking, camping, and outdoor life in general, to say nothing of the years I spent in the army. I was the one who led the songs in the dining hall and around the campfires and improvised military-style "shouts" for drills and hikes. Having a cabin of about 15 kids between five in the morning and seven in the evening, and a couple of counselors and junior counselors was an all-consuming job that took every minute of the day. The idea was to make it interesting and as much fun as possible for these kids who had just parted from their parents, probably for the first time in their lives.

At Juilliard the students were on their own, seeking their own goals, but at Rabbit Hollow, we were a staff pulling together for the common good, which was a different kind of experience. The New Hampshire hills were beautiful, and meeting a whole new bunch of people from all over was exhilarating. The campers were a challenge, but after a few days you got used to one another and generally had fun. I was one of the two dining-hall song leaders and I was really good. Every two weeks we sent the kids home and welcomed another batch. As a joint camp project, I directed a production of *H.M.S. Pinafore*, one of the summer's highlights.

There were hikes back and forth between the girls' and boys' camps, which were about three miles apart. At the end of the summer we were a happy, exhausted bunch. I don't remember what the pay was but it was very low—say about $150 for the summer.

My best buddy was a counselor named Bill Katz, a student at City College in New York. Bill introduced me to folk music. He knew chords on guitar and I was hooked. I started learning folk songs.

At the end of August, camp closed, and I was back in New York. The first thing I did was buy a cheap guitar at a pawnshop, and then I started preparing to depart for the University of Arizona in Tucson. I didn't know a soul in the entire region, nor had I been accepted at the school at the time of departure. It was a bit chancy, but I was game. I was a veteran, and the GI Bill allowed me to go to any school that would accept me. And Arizona was the Southwest, not the South.

# SOLFA 6

*la*

I BOUGHT A Trailways bus ticket and headed for the great outdoors. The trip took about two-and-a-half days. My first experience with open discrimination on the trip was at the bus stop in Joplin, Missouri, when the counter girl politely told me that she could not serve me at the counter. I knew that this was supposed to happen in the southern states, but it still left me with feelings of anger and frustration when I finally confronted it. The next major stop was in Tulsa, Oklahoma, and although *Oklahoma!* was the biggest hit on Broadway at the time, I was much less than enchanted when a counterman literally screamed in my face directing me to the side door for Colored.

After three cramped days on the bus, I finally arrived in Tucson. I checked the telephone directory and found a listing for an A.M.E. (African Methodist Episcopal) church and phoned. I told the minister why I was there. He invited me out, and I took a cab to the church. The minister welcomed me to Tucson, secured a room for me with one of his parishioners who lived on the edge of the desert, and arranged that I go the next day with his son, who was registering at the university as a freshman. At the school, although I lacked formal papers, they registered me under the GI Bill, pending receipt of my transcript from Juilliard. I was required to take a more academic program than before (this school after all was not music, although I remained a music major). I took voice, botany, Spanish, English, and a humanities course that dealt with literature, theatre, art, history, ethics, government and politics.

The University of Arizona was in Tucson, only about 50 miles from the Mexican border. Mexicans were the largest minority and blacks were a distinct minority with a segregated grammar school, but the high school was integrated because there were not enough black students to warrant a separate school.

While registering, I was invited to join the Canterbury Club, the Episcopal Church student center on campus. At the introductory gathering at the center, I noticed that I was the only black member of the group.

The University of Arizona was a fairly sophisticated school with a good academic rating, although it was set in the desert and foothills outside of town. Many of its 5,000 students were from out of state for a lot of reasons: its setting, leisurely pace, good winter climate, and dry therapeutic atmosphere for sufferers of asthma and arthritis. There appeared to be more wheelchair-bound students than on the average campus. But the university also had a good football team, the Wildcats. I would say that there were about 50 blacks on the campus, practically all from Arizona.

Although I would not be served a Coke at the drugstore outside of campus, everything on campus was OK. I was well received at the Canterbury Club and the students were bright, enthusiastic and open. I developed a few friendships and spent my time chatting, studying and participating in other activities. Sometimes, we went out on the desert for a picnic and spent the day playing games, eating and horsing around.

I became a volunteer acolyte for the little service we held each week in the chapel. During communion, the wine is sipped from a single chalice with just a slight turn of it and a rub with a cloth by the priest. I am sure that it was the first time that most of them had taken communion with a black. All went smoothly.

Before I went into the army I knew the words and music to just about every pop song by heart. Until World War II, pop songs were controlled by publishers mostly in the Brill Building, on Broadway at 49th Street. Songwriters came in, played their songs on the piano, and the publishers passed the lead sheets on to various artists and bandleaders. By the end of the 1930s most of the top Tin Pan Alley writers like Irving Berlin, Vincent Youmans, George and Ira Gershwin were swallowed up by Hollywood, to write musical extravaganzas starring Fred Astaire, Alice Faye, Dick Powell and Judy Garland.

After the war, with the rise of rhythm and blues, country, western and folk music, the pattern changed drastically. The "June-moon" format was changing to fit the real world. Hiroshima and Nagasaki, civil rights, war crimes tribunals, the murder of six million Jews, the state of Israel, the Korean War, the recall of General MacArthur. The songs said: "Where have all the flowers gone," "Hang down your head an' cry, Tom Dooley, Poor boy, you're goin' to die," "You lift sixteen tons, and what do you get, another day older and deeper in debt." There were songs from the French Resistance in World War II, songs of the Lincoln Brigade from the Spanish Civil War, trade union songs uniting the workers, black spirituals and work songs ("John Henry," the steel drivin' man) and "We Shall Overcome."

These songs captured the minds of some of the postwar generation because they had a social significance. The youth of America began to take themselves seriously in schools and on campuses, and political action groups sprang up, particularly around the presidential candidacy of Henry Wallace in 1948. Black people, white liberals and progressives took the first steps to meeting on common ground, in schools, in the workplace, and in the society at large.

Guitars and banjos started selling like hotcakes and it seemed that everyone—young and old—started taking guitar lessons. Burl Ives, the first big folk star, was concertizing all over. The Weavers were holding forth at the Village Vanguard, and Josh White was a regular at Café Society. Woody Guthrie was appearing at hootenannies and Sister Rosetta Tharpe was a hot item at village clubs. Richard Dyer Bennett brought his English ballads to the folk scene, and Andres Segovia, the Spanish guitarist, was practically worshipped.

At Arizona I settled into my studies, and spent most of my non-class time either in the library or at the Canterbury Student Center. I lived on the edge of town and came in to school each day on the bus. After a couple of weeks, the school offered me a place on campus. Three other black students from Phoenix and I were offered a room at the stadium dorm where the football team was housed. We were the first blacks to live on campus. The room had two double bunks, but it was on campus, which cut out travel. My roommates and I mostly used the room to sleep; it was too small for study with any real degree of comfort. I studied mostly at the center where I could usually listen to music in the background. I remember my favorite record was an instrumental version of "The Love Duet" from Richard Wagner's *Tristan und Isolde*.

I took my meals at the student union, which had a meal plan. The food was generally bad but wholesome, and relatively cheap. I met a black student who was taking a couple of classes at the university and who was confined to a wheelchair. She had crippling arthritis and her mother had to bring her to Arizona to keep her alive. Her mother was a professional cook, and once in a while they would invite me out to their place for dinner. I struck up a few good student friendships with the regulars at the center. Many of these students had never gone to school or socialized with a black person before and I was aware that they were generally enjoying the experience. I was bright, open and talented and knew my way around people, and I was cool.

As a student at Juilliard, New York (1946-48)

The Blue Angel, Chicago (1953)

New Year's Eve, Chicago (1951)

At the Village Vanguard (1954)

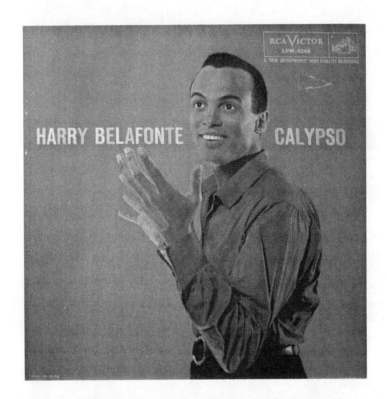

The first million-selling LP (1956)

Ballad for Bimshire,
Mayfair Theatre, N.Y. (1963)

Burgie's second album for Belafonte (1958)

Burgie's third album for Belafonte (1960)

Royal Philharmonic Orchestra album
of Burgie's songs (1983)

Irving and Page's wedding, Richmond, VA (May 1956)

Visiting London, England (1958)

Reception for Irving Burgie
at University in Rome, Italy (1958)

With his two sons, Irving Jr. and Andrew,
on vacation in Puerto Rico (1980)

Reception at the Burgie home for Amy Ashwood Garvey,
the first wife of Marcus Garvey and co-founder of the UNIA (1968)

Principals of the musical *Ballad for Bimshire*:
Miriam Burton and Frederick O'Neal.
O'Neal was the president of Actors' Equity.

The production team for the musical *Ballad for Bimshire*:
Irving Burgie, Ossie Davis, Sylvester Leaks,
(Above) Ed Cambridge, Ewart Guinier

Reception for Daisy Bates who led group of black children
into Little Rock High School under protection of the
National Guard as the nation watched

Paul O'Dwyer, President of the City Council,
N.Y., being greeted by Page Burgie
at a reception by CPR (1970)

I was a voice major at Arizona and I continued with the art songs repertoire, but I began, on the side, to practice my guitar and build my list of folk songs. My most interesting class was Humanities; it covered literature, culture and the social sciences. The downside was that the class was at one o'clock in the afternoon, and it got awfully hot. Traditionally, that was nap time in Arizona, before air conditioning. And, as I sat almost directly in front of the professor, who had a monotonous voice, I mastered the art of sleeping with my eyes open. But it was a good course.

I met a few of the black students on campus and we even tried to start a club, but it never really got off the ground. Possibly too few students, schoolwork—whatever, but it didn't happen. I was rather apathetic about botany and learning the names of all those plants. But I crammed and got the second highest mark in the class on the lab final; I got a B.

It was my first time at a school with a real campus, and I enjoyed rooting for the Wildcats in basketball and football. The Cleveland Indians' spring training camp was just outside Tucson, and once I met Larry Doby who was the first black player in the American League and a star for the Cleveland Indians. Just the year before, Jackie Robinson had broken the color line in the major leagues by joining the Brooklyn Dodgers. Satchel Paige, the black pitching legend, after a brilliant career in the Negro Leagues, was closing out his days pitching for Cleveland.

At the center one day I met a female student from Columbus, Ohio, who charmed me in an instant. After two minutes of conversation and a couple of smiles, I was hooked. By the next time I saw her, I was madly in love, and by the next day even more so. Our conversations hardly went beyond a few words, but that was enough. Of course, she had no idea what was going on in my mind, or at least she didn't let on that she did. Maybe she was thinking the same about me. We never dated or even talked outside the student center but, somehow, that arrangement seemed sufficient. I just decided to regard her as my girl, even if she didn't have a clue about it. Anyway, it was a nice way to feel about somebody. She seemed to have a boyfriend whom I saw with her from time to time on campus, but as far as I was concerned, he was just her chaperone, guarding her in my absence—which was most of the time. I had pleasant dreams. So much for love.

I practiced my guitar chords and was able to use folk themes for term papers in a couple of courses. Once settled in, the term moved along with the occasional picnics, nickel poker games, reading, and all the other stuff students used to do. Study and social life were generally centered at the student center. I'd go out to the desert once in a while to watch the famous golden Arizona sunsets—sunsets like the ones you saw in the magazine *Arizona Highways*.

The Arizona climate made no great difference to me vocally, although it did reduce my nasal congestion. I was now in my third year under the GI Bill and began to evaluate my position and my future more seriously. My interests and studies had been quite diverse, and though I was a voice major, I never really pursued a degree in voice, because I didn't think it would be of much use in the outside world. However, I had absorbed a lot of music and studies in the past four years. At the end of my year at Arizona, it felt like a pleasant and positive interlude in my march to "wherever."

I began to ponder my next move. I had one more year of eligibility under the GI Bill. I thought it would be best used in an urban environment where my artistic and job possibilities might be better. I chose to go to the University of Southern California in Los Angeles.

Meanwhile, I was invited to return to Camp Rabbit Hollow for the summer, so after a month at home and after checking out the folk scene in Greenwich Village, I left for Winchester, New Hampshire. During orientation week I saw many of the counselors from the prior summer, plus some new faces. I was happy to see that Bill Katz, my folk-song buddy, had returned. New season, new challenges, and new kids—here we go again. This summer was equally demanding. I directed *The Pirates of Penzance* for the season closer. On my days off, I usually went into the woods with my guitar.

After camp, I returned to New York, checked out the folk scene in the village again and got ready for my trip to Los Angeles. At that time, my brother Will at 21 was a social worker with lots of background in camping and scouting. While working for the New York City Mission Society and as Boys' Director at Camp Minisink, he went into the army (which had been integrated in 1948). He went to officer training school and became a second lieutenant in a tank battalion at Fort Hood, Texas. After the army, he worked for the Society while going to New York University, where he got a bachelor's degree in sociology. He went on to an illustrious career as Boys' Director of the Harlem Unit of the New York City Mission Society—a position he held throughout his life. He developed the New York City Mission Society Cadet Corps and built their drum and bugle corps to the level of national competition. The Cadet Corps appeared annually in revue at Madison Square Garden in New York. His work has touched the lives of thousands of children for almost 40 years.

At the end of August, I took the train from New York's Penn Station to Los Angeles. It was a two-and-a-half-day ride sitting up in coach. On the train I met Dottie Lane, a young black woman on vacation from New Jersey, and we made pleasant company on the trip, although it was quite cramped. I had a letter of introduction to a black minister who also owned an employment agency, which was adjacent to his house. His church was next door. He gave me a job keeping the grounds and the walks clean, and this went towards my room rent. U.S.C. was a large and well-endowed campus. The music department was formidable and so was the film department. Voice was my major and I studied with George Hultgren.

My landlord was a man of about 60, and the most self-centered, self-righteous, opinionated, deceitful, loathsome asshole that I had ever met, and I made a point of staying out of his way as much as possible. The fact that my room was in the building in the rear, which had a kitchen and a couple of other rental rooms, allowed me some privacy.

The tone at U.S.C. was quite a bit different from the University of Arizona. This was a large, impersonal place where it was much more difficult to establish friendships. However, I did meet Bill Sanford, a young black music student, who invited me up to Watts, which was part of the black ghetto of Los Angeles. He was the organist and choirmaster at a church that was rehearsing Handel's *Messiah* for Christmas, and I had sung it in the choir back home in Brooklyn. There was only a sprinkling of black students at U.S.C. because it was a private school with a higher tuition. There were many more black students at U.C.L.A., the state school across town. Outright racial taboos did not exist in Los Angeles as they did in some places in Tucson, Arizona. It was a big sprawling town with a sizeable black and Mexican community. I was somewhat surprised by the size of the "skid row" downtown. It seemed like half the hobos and derelicts in the country had come out to take advantage of the mild climate.

I met Lucille Clarke, who had done some clerical work for the minister. She was a former voice student and at times performed as a soprano soloist. One Sunday, she was the soloist at the minister's church and she invited me to attend. Lucille was an attractive woman in her late thirties who had studied voice and at one time was a singer with the Hall Johnson choir. She had two children who were already out in the world. She was doing part-time secretarial work when I met her. She lived alone in a one-family house and had a car. She was charming and wise, with a good sense of humor. We shared a common interest in music, were attracted to each other, and sort of became pals. We pooled what little resources we had and I generally had my evening meals at her house. I still had my room with the minister but, after a while, I only slept there. I spent most of my leisure time with Lucille, chatting, taking in a movie once in a while, or a concert or a program; but we spent hardly any money. I was studying for my classes, practicing my guitar, building repertoire, and we enjoyed each other's company.

The money that I had saved in the army and used to supplement my $75 a month GI Bill allotment was now drying up. I left school during the month of December to work at Christmas, hauling mail sacks for the post office. Still, I was able to get back to classes and make up my lessons by semester's end. Folk music kept moving on up and I managed to see Tennessee Ernie Ford in a show downtown when his recording of "16 Tons" was No.1.

I was now practicing my folk songs on a regular basis and I auditioned for a TV variety show contest that was headed by a well-known bandleader. I sang "John Henry" and "Wanderin'." I was chosen to go on the air to compete with several other contestants. The producers liked me and had already plotted that I would win the first three weeks leading up to the finals. A meter measured the audience applause to determine the winner each week. One of the contestants was a trumpet player who specialized in blowing mostly loud, high notes. The crew had me ahead on the applause meter, but in the final run-off, the audience preference was so obvious that if that trumpeter didn't win, there was going to be a riot. So much for my television debut.

In one of my English classes, I performed some folk songs, and the instructor recommended that I meet with the director of the college radio station KUSC. He was impressed with my work and gave me a half-hour program where I talked about folk music and sang songs once a week. Researching material, arranging, and program preparation on a weekly basis kept me hopping and motivated along with keeping up with my class work.

During the winter break I was invited by two students I knew from Tucson to attend their wedding, so I had a reunion with some of the gang from the previous year. I stayed at the newlyweds' house.

Lacking funds, I didn't get to see much of the glamorous Hollywood side of L.A., and I wasn't really that interested. I was able to take in a couple of sessions of the Coliseum Relays; U.S.C. was the host. I was the fastest kid in grammar school until my last year, so I liked to follow track. But, for the most part, it was me and my guitar. By now, I was getting fairly good.

Approaching the end of the spring semester Lucille had to give up her house, and she moved out to the San Fernando Valley with relatives. I went out one weekend at the end of the term for a farewell before I headed back east.

Lucille was the first woman that I had had an extended, almost day-to-day relationship with (seven months). We both understood, without saying, that the relationship would be a limited one, and we played it one month at a time. All in all it was positive for us both and we parted lovers and friends. We exchanged a postcard or two, and that was the end of it. We completely lost track of each other, but the memory is a pleasant one.

I took that two-and-a-half-day train ride back to New York, and to an uncertain future.

My brother Will was preparing to leave home for the army and officer candidate school. He offered me a summer job as a counselor at Camp Minisink in Port Jervis, New York.

While at Juilliard I studied mostly music-related subjects and languages. At Arizona it was English, humanities, biology, and language. By the time I left U.S.C. I had accumulated about 137 credits, but not concentrated in a discipline to warrant a bachelor's degree. My reasoning was that a degree in music would not be essential to my performing pursuits.

Camp Minisink was operated by the New York City Mission Society as their Harlem unit and was for black campers. They also operated Camp Sharperoon in Dover Furnace, N.Y., for their downtown unit, which was for white campers. The Minisink counselors were recruited mostly from the Harlem unit winter program and some from black colleges in the South. There was only one white counselor on the staff. It was a fairly large camp and had been around since the late 1930s. At Camp Minisink I was well received both as a counselor and folk singer, and was one of the leaders in the almost daily songfest.

Before I headed for the camp, I had spent the weekends of June performing in Greenwich Village at the fountain in Washington Square and had begun attracting my share of the crowd with my guitar and singing.

It was at Camp Minisink in that summer of 1950 that Harry Belafonte and I first met. He was passing through the area and spent the night at the Minisink lodge. He had recently made his first film *Bright Road* opposite Dorothy Dandridge and was beginning to make a stir generally. He was also singing jazz at the Royal Roost, a nightclub in New York. They asked Harry and me to do a number at the monthly birthday party in the dining-hall the next night. We met and rehearsed the next afternoon and that evening we did a duet on "John Henry" that really broke up the place. Of course, the young girls and counselors were practically passing out just looking at Harry. It was to be five more years before we got together professionally. After camp I returned to my mom's apartment in Brooklyn. I was offered a part-time job with the Minisink Townhouse program, which ran during the school year. The pay was low, but I managed.

Bill Katz, Dave Bromberg, and I got together on weekends at the square in the village and I was now practicing or doing research most of the time. That fall I auditioned at Café Society Downtown, one of the best-known clubs for folk music by such performers as Josh White, Richard Dyer Bennett, and Billie Holiday. They seemed to like me and called me back a couple of times to audition, but nothing came from it. But I began appearing on a few folk programs and hootenannies around town.

Gwen Struick, who was a teenager with a Unitarian group attached to Camp Rabbit Hollow a couple of years back, was now a student at Antioch College, a progressive liberal arts school in Yellow Springs, Ohio. The students spent part of the school year working on related jobs in various cities. Gwen got in touch with Bill Katz and me and met with students who were working and living around town. These students were primarily white middle-class kids with a couple of blacks among them, and we had a great time singing folk songs and creating mild havoc in general in various student apartments during the year. The students were generally above average and politically progressive.

Thurgood Marshall, the brilliant lawyer-strategist who served as legal director of the N.A.A.C.P from 1940 to 1961, had brought the Brown v. Board of Education to the Supreme Court. In 1954 the court would outlaw segregation throughout the school systems of the nation. Marshall of course went on to become the first black Supreme Court justice.

Various black writers, activists, and intellectuals, going back to the Harlem Renaissance of the 1920s and before, established the foundation that the civil rights movement was built on. During the 1920s the children of the first large migration of blacks who migrated north during World War I were able to attend public grammar and high schools, especially in major cities like New York, Detroit, Chicago, and Cleveland.

Richard Wright (1908-1960) became the first internationally recognized black writer in 1940 with the publication of his novel *Native Son* and his autobiography *Black Boy*. On the heels of Richard Wright came Ralph Ellison (1914-1994) with *Invisible Man* (1952). A decade before the Harlem Renaissance, Claude McKay, a Jamaican living in Harlem, wrote *Home to Harlem* and became the first black winner of the Pulitzer Prize.

Virtually all of the black writers of this "new awakening" were part of the political left including Wright, Ellison, Langston Hughes, Claude McKay and Walter White. Until the civil rights movement of the 1950s, the government of the United States upheld sorely outdated laws that discriminated against black Americans in a variety of ways, and these artists were among the most eloquent protesters. During the late 1940s and early 1950s, I read Richard Wright's *Native Son* and *Black Boy*, Ralph Ellison's *Invisible Man*, and Claude McKay's *Home to Harlem* among others, which, coupled with my own experiences, helped form the basis of my own socio-political thinking.

The Communist Party, which was a legitimate entity at the time, and the progressive movement in general sought to identify with the plight of the black masses, and many of the early pre-war and post-war black leaders were championed by the left.

After World War II, America found itself thrust into the position of leadership of the "Free World" and in possession of unpaid debts to its own short-changed social groups. Over the next 20 years America grappled with this task in various ways as these people asserted themselves seeking equality and representation in society, demanding civil rights, women's rights and gay rights and other social goals.

It was during these times that America took to the guitar and folk music. John and Alan Lomax, the folklorists, had discovered "Leadbelly" (Huddie Ledbetter), a repository of black folk culture with a driving delivery and presence. Because of his musical gifts he was pardoned by the governor of Texas and released in care of the Lomaxes, who brought him to New York where he starred at the Village Vanguard. His most famous song "Goodnight Irene" became No. 1 on the Billboard charts.

In the late 1940s, Burl Ives was the first nationally recognized folk singer, as he introduced such songs as "The Blue-Tail Fly" and "On

Top of Old Smokey" to mass audiences. Millions of young people and their parents began taking guitar lessons and learning the relatively simple chords that were required for the average folk song. Few of the folk songs went beyond four or five chords. Ives first sang in nightclubs, but quickly moved into major concert halls. "Tennessee" Ernie Ford, a Nashville style singer, made a national hit out of "16 Tons," the 1946 song written by Merle Travis.

The labor movement was a hotbed of the folk movement and such labor songs as "Joe Hill," "Union Maid" and "Picket Line Priscilla" became staples of folk singers. The black spiritual "We Shall Overcome" became the anthem at gatherings, meetings and demonstrations of all types. Work songs such as "John Henry" and "Jump Down, Turn Around" were sung all over the country.

The songs of the Abraham Lincoln Brigade, a contingent of American volunteers who went to fight in Spain during the Spanish Civil War in 1937, were popularized by Pete Seeger and the Weavers, the leading folk group of the late 1940s. They had a number one hit with "Tsena Tsena," a song derived from an Israeli folk dance. These groups were primarily left wing or "progressive," and protesting primarily against "the system." There was no end to the rallies, hootenannies and conferences, and the ordinary citizen seemed as involved as never before.

One day it dawned on me that I was a grown man still living in my mother's apartment and not paying my way. With the part-time job I had with the City Mission Society, I couldn't even afford to take a girl to a movie. I didn't even have a girlfriend who might miss me while I was gone. I began to feel sensitive about my present state. My few friends were mostly transients and out-of-towners whom I had met in school or at summer camps. I had very little contact with my old pre-war friends. We had all grown up. I was 26 years old and beginning to regard myself as an old young man. I was five years out of the army, five years of knocking around, studying, folk singing and playing for people where I found them.

I suddenly felt claustrophobic being in New York. It seemed like everybody comes to New York to seek his or her fortune, but me. I was born here. The fact was, I wasn't really making it, not at all. Everybody comes to New York—so I reasoned that I might do better going somewhere else.

Actually, I had been practicing my guitar and gathering material and folk songs for only three years, although, to me, it seemed like a long time. I guess I thought I had something to say—and I was a bit driven. With all my studies overseas in the army and four and a half years of schooling under the GI Bill, I still didn't have the credentials to do anything specific.

I was watching the Arthur Godfrey TV show one day, and I saw this black singing group called the Karamu House Quartet perform. Karamu House was a settlement house in Cleveland started by the Jellifs, a white couple. They were making a name for themselves through the settlement with its musical theater and cultural program in the black community. I was impressed with the performance of the quartet, and got the idea that Karamu House and Cleveland might be a good place to continue my development.

But first I returned to Camp Minisink for the summer of 1951. It was a hardworking summer, and to close the season I directed the camp's production of *H.M.S. Pinafore*, which I had done at Camp Rabbit Hollow the previous two years.

While preparing to go to Cleveland, I saw that Chicago was not that much farther away. Chicago being a bigger town, I figured I might as well go there, since I didn't know anybody in either place. In September, a friend of one of my cousins was driving from New York to join his outfit in Texas, and he gave me a lift as far as Gary, Indiana, a suburb of Chicago. From there I got a lift in a *Chicago Defender* newspaper van, the city's black paper. The driver dropped me off in front of the black YMCA in the heart of the Chicago's south side black neighborhood.

Right away I got a job as a bus boy, cleaning and setting up tables in the La Salle hotel in downtown Chicago. The pay was low, but they also gave you a meal each day, which came in handy. I worked only one week at the La Salle, because I got a job at the post office, which was giving preference to veterans. The only hitch was that it was on the midnight shift. But I needed a good paying job for a while, so I took it. I worked that midnight shift for three months and saved as much as I could. During the day I mainly practiced my guitar and studied. The money was OK, but it was a drag for a young man of 27 who came to Chicago to seek his fortune to be holed up on a job five nights a week.

I didn't know anyone in Chicago, but I had heard of the Club DeLisa on the south side that featured a chorus line and headliners from the black nightclub circuit. I would visit the club on weekends and have a beer or two. Joe Williams, the black singer often performed there. (He later became famous with Count Basie and as a single act.)

I had been three months on the job and I hadn't had a chance to meet anyone in Chicago and then, finally, I met the brother of Miles Davis, who was also staying at the "Y." He took me around the block to meet Margaret Burroughs, the director of the South Side Community Art Center, a project left over from the W.P.A. It was in a converted mansion.

It happened also to be New Year's Eve, and Margaret invited me to a party that night on the white north side, at the home of Ed Gurfaine. He and his wife Joyce were two of Margaret's biggest supporters, and Ed owned a highly successful public relations business, and moved primarily in progressive circles. It was a great interracial party and I had a ball. I played my guitar and sang in Chicago for the first time as everybody joined in. It was a dancing, laughing New Year's Eve crowd that was "just what the doctor ordered."

Margaret lived in a converted carriage house behind an old mansion that had become the Quincy Club, a lodging for working members of the Brotherhood of Sleeping Car Porters. Margaret was a high school art teacher and artist in her thirties and was married to Charles Burroughs. She had a ten-year-old daughter, Gail, from a previous marriage to the artist Bernard Goss. There was a bohemian air about the place and people seemed to come and go constantly.

Most of the black creative people of Chicago came through the art center at one time or the other, and people like the poet Gwendolyn Brooks, Charles White, Elizabeth Catlett, Elizia Cortor, Jacob Lawrence, and Paul Robeson were all friends and contemporaries.

It was Margaret who first told me about Du Sable, a black Haitian who founded the city of Chicago. He first went to Canada, and then established a trading post on what became the Chicago River. (The high school where Margaret worked was named after DuSable). Margaret was plain speaking, intelligent, and she worked tirelessly with black children and adults to project the consciousness of progress and race. She was active in left-wing politics and a leading agitator for civil rights in the area.

The community center was a meeting ground for a variety of artistic pursuits—dance, theatre, painting, sculpture, writing, as well as good conversation. All of this was carried out on a shoestring basis, but it brought together like-minded, serious, creative black people at a time when they were sowing the seeds of the civil rights movement. They were writing, reading, sharing, arguing, and forging a new way for themselves. And I was among them. The progressives welcomed me to Chicago and I played and sang for several trade union functions and house parties. It was small-time stuff, but those $20 and $25 gigs were welcome. Margaret and I became fast friends, and I practically became part of the family.

I got a job paying $40 a week in a spice factory—moving boxes around on a cart. But I kept my shirt pocket full of slips of paper with things I had to study and songs I had to memorize. So the time wasn't wasted.

Just about that time, Gwen Struick from Antioch College came to Chicago to do a three-month work stint as part of her school curriculum. She introduced me to Will Jones, a black man who lived at the University of Chicago Settlement House.

The settlement house movement was developed by educated white women who wanted to make a contribution to society in the days when women did not compete with men in the marketplace. They sought funds from wealthy businessmen and philanthropists to develop these service areas in working-class communities. I had heard about the settlement house movement in my humanities class back at the University of Arizona.

The first settlement house was started by Jane Addams in Chicago and was called Hull House. The movement was an immediate success and settlement houses began to spring up in cities all over America. Mary McDonald, a disciple of Jane Addams, established the University of Chicago Settlement House (later called McDonald House) in the stockyards area of west Chicago. It was a decidedly blue-collar area that carried the stench of animal blood throughout the neighborhood at killing time. The settlement served the community in many ways, with classrooms, kindergartens and courses in crafts, sewing, cooking, maternity, sanitation and first aid. It also provided counseling and ran civic meetings and lobbying groups. Students in social work and sociology also lived there.

Will Jones invited me to the settlement for dinner. He had a degree from Roosevelt College in Chicago and was then working as a welder. He was bright, informed, and friendly. At dinner there was a girl, Liz Liau, from Hawaii, another girl from Smith College in Massachusetts, a Mexican couple, two more girls and two guys—all white.

I was offered a room there and quickly accepted. The rooms were situated on two floors with two baths on a floor, and the building was co-ed. The fee was low, and you volunteered service on the switchboard and stoking the furnace. Will Jones had a good record collection and was just a couple of doors down the hall from me, so I dropped by often to talk and listen. Liz from Hawaii's room was directly opposite mine, and she was friendly. Her boyfriend did not live at the settlement.

Everyone was cordial, and the evening meal was the high point of living at the settlement. During the day I worked part-time to pay my expenses. My main hangout nights and weekends was on the south side at Margaret's house or across the street from her at the center.

The progressive community passed the word around about my performing, and I was invited to play at gatherings and house parties almost every weekend. A sprinkling of interracial couples showed up at these events, and race was not a negative factor.

Living at the settlement house and hanging out at the center and Margaret's house seemed like a good thing to me, and it fell right in with my studies and folk singing. I was gaining in confidence, maturing politically, and feeling good about my progress. In the spring, the Southside Community Art Center, with the support of other progressive groups, sponsored me in a concert of folk songs in downtown Chicago at the Art Institute. That did a lot to establish me in the cultural life of the city.

In my studies at college, I had read about the group of writers called the "Chicago School," which included Carl Sandburg, Sherwood Anderson, Theodore Dreiser, and Edgar Lee Masters. They portrayed the starkness and ruggedness of American cities and small towns. I had a feeling of being in step and allied with the common man in a way that was new to me. And it felt good.

I was asked to return to Camp Minisink as a unit head that summer, and accepted. My brother Will, who had been boys' director of the camp, was now a lieutenant in the army. It was my fifth consecutive year of summer counseling and it went well.

At the end of summer camp I contemplated my next move. My year away from New York put me out of touch with things. Although I was poor and jobless I felt a strong urge to return to my situation in Chicago with Margaret, the art center, the settlement house and my new progressive friends. So, my guitar and I took off, returned to the settlement house, and picked up where we had left off.

Back in Chicago I continued to play for gatherings here and there, but I had to get a real job, so I went to work for a metal tube maker and was back on the midnight shift. I inspected and measured the tubes as they were turned out on the lathes. Luckily I had learned to use a micrometer, the measurement tool, in high school. I hated working at night, because it isolated me from my friends and the art center. At about 4 AM I would get so sleepy I could hardly keep my eyes open; then at 7 AM, I would leave work, go home, and start waking up as the sun came up.

In January, after about two months on the job, I got a call from Jimmy Payne, who had a dance studio on the south side. A new nightclub called the Blue Angel, that had a Caribbean theme, was opening on Rush Street in downtown Chicago, and I was hired as the calypso singer. Velyn and Laverne, a dance team, came from New York. Raquel, a Mexican singer from Chicago, and Grace Nichols, a dancer from Jimmy Payne's studio (she later became Nichelle Nichols of the *Star Trek* series) were also performing. A five-piece combo rounded out the show. We were well received, and the club did good business.

It was my first real nightclub gig and I made about $170 a week, which was a lot of money to me. I worked six nights a week with Sundays off (except for special parties). I moved out of the settlement house into a one-room apartment and was able to save a few bucks each week.

As the club became more popular, I became more featured as the calypso singer. The whole interest in calypso had been building

slowly since the end of World War II. In the 1950ss Americans
started visiting the Caribbean in large numbers, and many came
back humming calypso ditties that originated primarily in Trinidad.
The songs were sung and danced at the tourist hotels and clubs
springing up all over the Caribbean. Errol Flynn, the movie star,
and Noel Coward were leaders of the jet set that drew the tourists to
the islands. Most of these songs were double-entendre, with strong
sexual undertones.

The only island song that ever made the US charts before was the
Andrew Sisters singing "Rum and Coca-Cola" right after the war.
Probably the Andrew Sisters themselves were not aware of the "double"
meaning in the song:

> "Rum and Coca Cola
> Go down Point Kumana
> Both mother and daughter.
> Working for the Yankee Dollar."

Americans were stationed in Trinidad during the war and Point Kumana
was actually the red light district of Port of Spain, the capital.

The tourist heard songs like "The Big Bamboo" and "Don't Touch
My Tomatoes" and "I Left Her Behind for You":

> "I kissed her hand
> I kissed her lips
> And I left her behind for you."

I knew many of these tourist favorites and sang them in my act along
with Caribbean folk songs. All this was a part of good-natured fun
as the tourists drank daquiris, rum punch, and Cuba libres, and
watched the shimmy dancers, fire-eaters and limbo dancers going
under the bar.

Being at the club six nights a week kept me busy but I continued to practice and research song material—now concentrating on the West Indies.

A young Trinidadian of East Indian background who was a student at the University of Chicago came to the club and was interested in the folk culture of the Caribbean. He had some material and several recordings, and I studied them. I had been researching American folk songs for about five years, and I now was dealing with the culture of my mother, who came from Barbados. There were merengues from Santo Domingo, mentos from Jamaica, work songs, ring games, shouts, ceremonials and rituals from Haiti. Meanwhile the folk movement in general was growing throughout the country. Katherine Dunham created a sensation introducing the folk and ritual dancing of the Caribbean in nightclub and concert appearances, and was followed by Pearl Primus from Trinidad and Jean Léon Destiné from Haiti.

With my progressive friends and associates in the civil rights movement, my interest in Caribbean culture and music went beyond that of the typical tourist double entendre, risqué tunes that projected West Indians as happy-go-lucky, irresponsible people.

I began to think about the culture of the islands and about the trials and aspirations in the everyday lives of the people. The rhythms and movement of West Indians were being exploited but they did not have a real voice beyond the bar room. The West Indians I knew, my mother, my aunts, uncles, and cousins were mostly poor, frugal, struggling people and life was not a joke.

Before Columbus, Caribe and Arawak Indians inhabited the islands. In the ensuing years the Spanish, British and French claimed most of the islands, and eventually killed off the Indians, and brought in people from Africa as slaves to work in the burgeoning sugar cane fields starting in the 1500s. The plantations were owned mostly by absentee landlords in Europe and operated for them by indentured servants.

I am sure that at least some of my popularity at the Blue Angel was that the audience could understand my English, which I gave only a slight island accent. They would have been hard-pressed to understand most of the native calypsonians. As a matter of fact, each payday we would end the second show and take particular delight in changing the last line in the chorus to "Kiss my ass Fardulli" (the owner of the club). The audience would be clapping and laughing, and as we used a heavy West Indian accent, they could not understand us. But all in all, my relationship with the owners was a good one. They told me I could work there as long as I wanted.

It was the early 1950s, and blacks had begun to assert themselves into the fiber of America. Ralph Bunche was a mediator at the United Nations. Josephine Baker made a triumphal return from Paris with an American tour. Ray Robinson was regarded as the greatest fighter, pound for pound, ever, and Leontyne Price was the new diva at the Metropolitan Opera.

I was making an adequate salary and was well established in my job, although working six nights a week was a bit confining. I continued my folk music research and studies of the Caribbean.

After four months at the club, I began to think about trying New York again. I felt that Chicago was OK, but you really have to make it in New York. I gave the club notice and left for New York after a six-month run.

By then the club had built a reputation and was hiring acts out of New York. I had just learned to drive and bought a second-hand car, my first, at age 29. I had motor trouble outside Philadelphia on my way to New York and had to leave the car and take a train into New York. It was August and I went to Camp Wingdale, a progressive interracial adult resort in upstate New York. There I met Bob Nemeroff and his wife Lorraine Hansbury (who wrote *Raisin in the Sun* a few years later, the first Broadway play written by a black). Julian Mayfield, a gifted young novelist, was also on the staff. They were doing a production called *I.R.T. Pinafore*, a workers' version of the Gilbert and Sullivan piece. The tenor had an impacted tooth and could not sing so I was asked to substitute; I learned the part in four days.

I visited Camp Minisink for a weekend on my way back from Camp Wingdale. My brother was getting married and he planned to live at home for a while, so I moved out into a rented hall room of an apartment in Harlem. I got a job in the mailroom of the headquarters of the Girl Scouts of America on the east side of Manhattan. Then I looked up my Haitian godparents, whom I hadn't seen in many years, and took some notes on Haitian folklore and voodoo ceremonies. As I was walking down the street in Greenwich Village one day I heard the sounds of someone practicing a guitar from an open window on the first floor. I went around and knocked on the door and introduced myself to Ferman Phillips. (He, Bill Attaway and Harry Belafonte had owned the Sage restaurant in the village a couple of years earlier.) He let me in and I played some songs for him. He was impressed and gave me the name of his guitar teacher, Jean Murai.

Jean Murai was a Jewish schoolteacher in her forties who had recently become a folk singer. She made a living playing and singing for progressive Jewish groups. Jean had also started a group called the Latin American Cultural Society, an interracial group made up of about 15 people, mostly Puerto Rican, Dominican, and Cuban.

Jean lived on West 21st Street in the Chelsea district of Manhattan. We met regularly at her apartment. She had done research in the Hispanic Caribbean and had collected a lot of material and songs that we practiced and developed. Sometimes the ensemble was invited to perform for schools and progressive groups. Mona Finkelstein, who was also a teacher, a contemporary, and a good friend of Jean's, lived in the same building and was a member of the society. She and I became good friends. She lived alone in her apartment and was a very bright and engaging woman. As one of the teachers subpoenaed by the House Un-American Activities committee who pleaded the Fifth Amendment,

Mona was suspended by the Board of Education (some years later they were all reinstated and given back pay).

M.C.A. (Music Corp. of America), the booking agency, would call me from time to time to do club dates for private parties and corporate functions. At one party held at the Astor Hotel, I was paired with a pianist named Herb Levy. He was a Jamaican, about 50, and had been in the musicians' union for years as a pianist. He knew a lot about the old songs of Jamaica. I arranged a meeting with him later, only to find out that Herb also played the pennywhistle (a little tin whistle) as a hobby. Herb's playing took me by surprise. He was amazing. Right away I got the idea of starting a group. I got Ozzie Bayez, a young Dominican from the cultural society on bongos, me on the guitar and lead vocals, and Al Lindo, a young Jamaican on maracas. I put together a program of calypso songs from Trinidad, mentos from Jamaica, rituals from Haiti and a few Hispanic songs from Santo Domingo, Cuba, and Puerto Rico. We played at a couple of affairs in the village and went over well.

Stinson Records, a folk recording company in the village, invited us to record an album. Earl Robinson, the gifted left-wing balladeer and composer of such songs as "Ballad for Americans" and "The House I Live In," arranged an audition with Max Gordon, owner of the Village Vanguard. At the same time Earl introduced me to a Jamaican folklorist and actress, Louise Bennett, who had just arrived in New York after studying at the Royal Academy of Arts in London.

I worked over a few things with Louise and had her join us for a couple of numbers and street cries at the audition. Max Gordon hired the group on the spot and gave us two weeks to get ready. We spent the time blending Louise into the group and working in some of her material. She was a plump, jolly, attractive woman, who dressed in Jamaican folk garb, and cut an imposing figure. Herb Levy was a fine musician and took some really artful solos that blended in beautifully with the guitar and drums. Our choral harmony and my lead singing rounded out the group.

The group was well received at the Vanguard. It was my first regular club appearance in New York, and it felt good. "Lord Burgess (Max Gordon gave me the name) and the Sun Islanders" was the first Caribbean-style group to come along, so we were a novelty. We spent six weeks at the Vanguard, but the group didn't really jell, and Louise's manager entertained the idea of her going out as a single. Also the idea of paying four people for one act was not attractive to club owners.

My name began to get around, and I was able to get a few single gigs through M.C.A. I was invited to do a solo concert at the library in Lenox, Mass., where the Tanglewood music festival was held each summer, with the Boston Symphony in residence. After the concert, I was invited to appear at various resorts in the area, such as Festival House and Music Inn. I sang a mix of folk songs and my Caribbean material, and became popular. I would appear every weekend at a different resort. They treated me as a guest and I fit in quite well. I made several friends. The guests were primarily weekenders who came up from New York for the Boston Symphony Orchestra programs in the big shed at Tanglewood, or to attend the Summer Jazz Festival at Music Inn. The Berkshires region was beautiful, with attractions like the Shaker Village Museum and the Jacob's Pillow Dance Festival.

When I returned to the city in the fall, I found a large front room that I rented from Johnny Williams. My new place had a large fireplace and was located in the heart of Greenwich Village on West 4th Street between 6th Avenue and MacDougal Street. It was on the third floor above a bar and grill called Chantilly. I shared the bath in the apartment with Johnny and another roomer who lived in the rest of the apartment. I don't know how Johnny came by the apartment but he was our landlord. He was a fairly pleasant brown skin guy, about 35, who talked a great deal about his French girlfriend who had just gone back to Paris. She had taught him a few French words that he threw around every once in a while. He played tennis on weekends, he had a job, but I never did know what he did. He had a good sense of humor and we got along well. I paid $75 a month for my rent. Gene Brintle also rented a room from Johnny at the other end of the apartment. Gene was a soft-spoken white man about 40 from Georgia with a southern drawl. He worked as a machinist and seemed something of a misfit in the village. Nevertheless, he was pleasant, agreeable, and fairly bright and people seemed to like him. He met a rather wild skinny black woman at a local bar and used to go barhopping with her on weekends. But during the week he went to work. Kenny Bell, a friend of Johnny, our landlord, would drop in often just to shoot the breeze. He was a short, stout, balding man about 60 from somewhere in the West Indies, who liked to drink, had a good mind, and could sometimes wax philosophical. From time to time the four of us had some freewheeling gab sessions.

The pedestrian traffic was enormous on weekends and the village teemed with life. I was only a block away from Washington Square Park and New York University. There were straight bars, gay bars, and coffee shops everywhere, many featuring folk singers, blues singers and poets.

I fixed up my room and painted it. I had a friend put up some curtains and a bedspread, and my room became an attractive studio. I started inviting my new friends from Tanglewood, and sometimes there were as many as 40 people in my room. I also began teaching folk guitar to a few students. About once a month I would have a soirée and charge a few bucks a head. It was good fun, with folk songs, conversation, and meeting people for an invited-only crowd. In the meanwhile I still hung out with Mona and The Latin American Cultural Society.

At Festival House I had met some people from Nassau County on Long Island. They set up a folk guitar class for me and would meet in a different person's home each week. I would show them techniques on the guitar, and after the lesson we would always sing and try out songs. The host would provide a collation. It was a unique group: Jewish, middle class, with children, merchant class, and living well. We became friends.

(After Page and I got married in 1956, we were often dinner guests at their homes and some of these friendships lasted for many years).

There had been several incidents of blacks protesting racial discrimination on buses and trains in the south, especially in interstate commerce during the 1950s. It came to a head with Rosa Parks not giving up her seat to a white man in 1955 in Montgomery, Alabama. The black community organized and began a bus boycott that lasted for more than a year. The year before, in the Brown v. Board of Education ruling, the US Supreme Court had ruled that "separate but equal" education of black children was unconstitutional. This set blacks and liberal whites all over the country gearing up for the coming confrontations, sit-ins, and freedom rides. The NAACP, and even churches, began to take on a militant air.

The militant wing of the NAACP became the Student Nonviolent Coordinating Committee (SNCC), which was led by Stokley Carmichael, Rap Brown, and other black students, mainly from southern colleges. Civil rights activity and protest sprang up in cities and towns all over America. There was a terrific groundswell and fervor that gripped the black community who had suffered as second-class citizens all their lives. The man in the street came forward, and he put it on the line.

I was asked to appear on several programs as a folk singer. I did a few gigs for industrial shows, because calypso singers were often asked to extemporize on various subjects, in rhyme, and I would build a song around the company or the product. But work was sporadic, and I was still poor and struggling to pay the rent.

People's Artists, a left-wing booking agency, got me a gig in New Jersey on an egg farm for $25 for New Year's Eve. I was too poor to turn it down. But the people were nice to me and I was part of an enjoyable New Year's Eve. That night, there was a frost, and the farmers had to light smudge pots in the sheds where the eggs were stored. The pots malfunctioned, and the next morning they discovered hundreds of eggs had been covered with soot. The community spent New Year's Day

1955 washing and wiping every single egg, one by one. I was asked to return to the Blue Angel in Chicago in March for a two-month run. It was nice seeing Margaret and the gang at the South Side Art Center again. However, I didn't have much time to hang out as I worked six nights a week.

Paul Robeson was a favorite target of the F.B.I., particularly because he advocated friendship with the Soviet Union in the middle of the Cold War. Robeson was scheduled to perform a concert at the Chicago Opera House. There was a strong protest from the right and the Opera House cancelled the concert. After much deliberation, it was decided that Robeson would appear at a public concert in Washington Park in Southside Chicago. Margaret was on the organizing committee and a close friend of Robeson. Several artists were asked to perform on a hastily put together outdoor platform. Margaret asked me to do a number on the program, and I agreed. Although the public address system left a lot to be desired, the concert went on (because of this appearance, and my previous appearance at Camp Wingdale in *I.R.T. Pinafore*, I was visited by the F.B.I. a couple of years later).

J. Edgar Hoover, the director of the F.B.I. during the civil rights movement, seemed to make little distinction between the people trying to overthrow the government and the activists and leaders of the movement. He harassed and treated them all as subversives.

Despite their status, and perhaps due to their long tenure in this country, blacks have always been loyal to the US and its promise of deliverance of freedom and equality to all its citizens. After Abraham Lincoln signed the Emancipation Proclamation ending slavery in 1863, more than 200,000 blacks, encouraged by Fredrick Douglass and other black leaders volunteered as soldiers in the Union Army.

The fact is that blacks, both slave and free, were several generations in the US at the time the Constitution was written in 1787. Blacks were the largest single group of immigrants to come to these shores, though they came against their will, shackled as slaves. The great European immigration did not materialize until the 19th and 20$^{th}$ centuries from Ireland, Italy, Germany, and eastern Europe. By then, most blacks could claim several generations of kin born in America.

I returned to New York after my two-month run at the Blue Angel and received a call from M.C.A. to meet a woman who was looking for Caribbean talent for her club Malayan Lounge in Miami Beach, on the 79$^{th}$ Street Causeway. She chose me to head a five-piece combo that she had picked out the same day. She was a Canadian and was impressed by my general manner, besides my performing attributes. I rehearsed with the combo for a few days, and then we flew down to Miami. Florida at the time was Jim Crow—separate facilities for blacks and whites, but the club owner was able to get us suitable lodging just down the street from the club on a property that she owned.

She treated me well, but the combo really couldn't cut it musically. After a week, she sent them back to New York and asked me to front the "Lord Flea" group from Jamaica. Lord Flea was lead singer and guitarist. Pork Chops was something of a visual comic who could play the banjo over his head and behind his back. Largie was on maracas, and Tony was on conga. The group looked a bit rough; they had come straight out of the hills of rural Jamaica. Only Tony could read and write, and he read them their mail and answered it. Lord Flea had made a name as a result of a couple of recordings. His musicians were good lounge entertainers and teamed with me on some vocals, and with me carrying the patter, we made an entertaining turn. Bahama Moma, an exotic dancer, was also on the bill.

Just before leaving New York, I had had lunch with an old friend from the Camp Minisink staff, Page Turner, who had graduated from Virginia Union Theological Seminary and was hired by the New York City Mission Society as a social worker. We enjoyed the conversation, and I promised to write her from Miami, which I did.

While in Miami, M.C.A. booked me for a single-day electrical industry convention on Fishers Island, off the coast of Connecticut. After performing and eating lobster all day (my first lobster), I returned to Miami just in time to make the show the next night. After expenses, I only cleared about $200, but the extra money was welcome. The gig was to end the first week in August, but after six weeks, the club owner tried to renege on my last week's pay. So I went to the musicians' local (segregated in Miami) and they got me my money. All in all it was a good stay and I learned a bit more about Jamaican folklore working with Flea and his group. (Two years later Lord Flea and his group were featured on the Perry Como TV show in New York. Flea died of leukemia shortly afterward.)

# SOLFA 7

*ti*

WHEN I RETURNED to New York I got a call from Bill Attaway, who had learned about me through Velyn and La Verne, the dance team I had worked with in Chicago. He was a writer who had done some TV scripts and a novel, and at that time was working for Harry Belafonte. Harry had just signed to do a couple of shots on the *Colgate Comedy Hour*, and Bill was looking for material. The CBS *Colgate Comedy Hour* was challenging the Sunday prime time dominance of the *Ed Sullivan Show* and hired several stars to fill slots on the program from week to week. Their first show was to be centered on the "John Henry" legend, and the second was to be on a Caribbean theme.

I met Bill at his flat in Manhattan, and I played and sang some of my songs. He was impressed. On the spot, he called Belafonte in San Francisco and suggested that they change the first show for Colgate from "John Henry" to a Caribbean format. Belafonte returned to New York a few days later. I played the material for him, and they decided then and there to do the Caribbean show around my music.

I was elated by all these events. When I returned from Miami I was invited to share the apartment of one of my friends from the Latin American Cultural Society, Montey Martinez, who was Puerto Rican and worked for the city subway system. Montey was easy going and friendly and a good friend of Jean Murai. The apartment was on Manhattan Avenue and 106th Street in a low-rent, mostly Hispanic part of Harlem. Like most parts of New York, the roaches there were constant adversaries.

Upon my return to the city, I looked up Page Turner and began to have lunch with her a couple of times a week. She lived at the black Y.W.C.A. in Harlem. The women had private rooms and invited guests were entertained in the common living room. I visited her at the "Y" once in a while. (Michael Olatunji, the African percussionist, and I became friends because he was courting his wife-to-be, Amy, at the "Y" at the same time.)

Harry Belafonte and I hit it off well, and I was certainly encouraged to be working on a network TV show. Harry had a nightclub engagement in Boston for two weeks. Bill went along with him to work on the Caribbean script to be built around my songs. But I was not invited. I didn't know anything about how royalties worked, but I naively told Bill that I wanted a guarantee from Harry of at least $500 for my songs being in the show. Bill said that Harry said yes.

Music publishing became more and more lucrative as the performing rights societies grew. ASCAP (American Society of Composers, Authors, and Publishers) and BMI (Broadcast Music Incorporated) collected and paid royalties from the songs being played on the radio, on television, and in concerts and cabarets—wherever music is played in the US. There were sister societies in countries all over the world that collected the proceeds of US copyrights from foreign sub-publishers: In England (PRS), France (SACEM), Germany (GEMA), Japan (JASRAC) and others. In turn, the American societies provided the service for the foreign societies. The business of commercial licenses also became significant as businesses used more and more popular songs to advertise products of all kinds on radio and TV. The biggest license I have ever gotten ($350,000) was for the use of "Day-O" by Daewoo, the Korean automobile company, in a TV commercial in Germany for one year in 1996.

I had learned something about the copyright game when I lived at the "Y" in Chicago back in 1951. A guy wrote a song and asked me to make a "demo" for him. He also asked me to help him get a copyright. I contacted the Library of Congress in Washington, got the forms, and registered the song as an unpublished copyright. This was the best way of guarding your rights before publication. I used this method to safeguard my work before I submitted it to the *Colgate Comedy Hour* and the *Calypso* album of Harry Belafonte. In those days many writers were being cheated by music publishers and producers, aided and abetted by the business naïveté of the horde of young new songwriters eager to get into the burgeoning music publishing houses. I was being extra careful. It paid off.

When Bill and Harry returned from Boston the Colgate show went into rehearsal. The day before the show went on the air, I was asked by the station to sign a release to allow my copyrighted songs to be used. After consulting with Harry, I agreed to give Bill Attaway 20 percent of five songs, including "Day-O," because Bill had altered the lyrics to fit the script. And I signed.

The show was a smash, and it set the industry buzzing. From the opening song, "Day-O," the show clicked. Belafonte went into the Starlight Roof of the Waldorf Astoria right after the show, and we started putting an album together. During the next month, I wrote three more songs that went into the album with "Day-O." That gave me a total of eight of the eleven songs in the album.

A year before I had been working on a song for my own act, which I called "Jamaica Farewell." I included it in the songs under consideration for the new Belafonte album, and he immediately fell in love with it. The song was also unusual in that the title does not appear in the song. We discussed this and decided to keep the name as it was. Belafonte recorded it on the *Calypso* album, and it became a tremendous singles hit afterwards. Belafonte made it his theme song and has sung it in all his concert and club appearances since then. Along with "Day-O," it became his theme song.

## JAMAICA FAREWELL

by Irving Burgie

1.  Down the way, where the nights are gay
    An' the sun shines daily on the mountaintop
    I took a trip, on a sailing ship
    An' when I reached Jamaica, I made a stop.

    Chorus:
    But I'm sad to say, I'm on my way
    Won't be back for many a day
    My heart is down, my head is turning around
    I had to leave a little girl in Kingston Town.

2.  Sounds of laughter everywhere
    An' the dancing girls swaying to and fro
    I must declare that my heart is there
    Tho' I've been from Maine to Mexico

3.  Down at the market you can hear
    Ladies cry out while on their heads they bear
    Ackie, rice, salt fish are nice
    An' the rum is fine any time of year

Harry Belafonte and the songs of *Calypso* were a boon to the fast growing Caribbean tourist industry, which was spurred by greatly increased air traffic after the war. Tourists literally flocked to such relatively close islands as Jamaica, the Bahamas, Antigua, Haiti, Barbados, Puerto Rico, Grenada, and of course Cuba. The *Calypso* album became No. 1 in most of Europe, Asia, Africa and the Caribbean. There were "covers" (native language recordings) by leading artists in just about every country. There were also many "covers" of the songs by artists in the US. The *Calypso* album itself became the first LP to sell a million copies. It was number one on the Billboard charts for 32 weeks and remained one of the Top 100 albums for 99 weeks. All this activity was reflected in my royalties for the songs in the year 1956: today's equivalent of more than a million dollars. "Day-O," "Jamaica Farewell," and "Island in the Sun" remained Belafonte's top three songs for his entire 50-year career.

The album was recorded at Webster Hall, which had just been acquired by RCA and converted into a recording studio because of its excellent acoustics. Tony Scott was the musical director and the musicians were top-notch: a chorus of about 20 of the best voices around; Millard Thomas on guitar; Franz Casseus, the Haitian guitarist who played those beautiful interludes in the song "Jamaica Farewell"; Norman Keenan on bass.

So much time was spent with the band on the first six numbers that we had to rush out the last five songs with me, Casseus, and Thomas on guitars, Norman on bass, and three guys on rhythm, all with "head" arrangements (playing chords without written music). Belafonte sang lead and I sang with him on the chorus of "Jamaica Farewell," "Come Back Liza," "I Do Adore Her" and "Dolly Dawn." On "Dolly Dawn," I just picked the name Dolly Dawn out of the nightclub section of the daily paper, and wrote a song about her—all from my imagination. My Dolly Dawn was an uninhibited dancer.

## DOLLY DAWN

by Irving Burgie

When Dolly hear them sound the drum
Up she jump and she holler, "Here I come."
(Repeat)
Chorus:
'Cause she gonna dance, she gonna sing
She gonna cause the rafters to ring. (Repeat)

(I met the real Dolly Dawn, the cabaret singer, 28 years later at a reception given for me by Cherry Lane Music, my publishers, at the Songwriters Hall of Fame to commemorate my songs having sold more than 100-million records.)

Until the royalties really started coming in, I was still poor and sharing an apartment with Montey in Spanish Harlem. I still had my class out on Long Island, and a gig here and there. The songs in the *Calypso* album were put in Clara Music Publishing Corp., named after Julie Belafonte's mother. Actually, there was only a one-page letter agreement that I had signed covering all the songs.

Clara Music Publishers had a few token copies of sheet music of several of my songs printed, but that (I found out) was only to satisfy the publisher's obligation under the contract, "to publish." I began to realize some time later, after doing a survey of music stores, that the sheet music was never put on sale. By the publisher doing this, my authorship of these songs (even after 50 years) was obliterated.

In 1965, nine years after the publication of the album *Calypso*, a formal contract was signed. In 1957 I had become a member of the Song Writers Guild (formerly Song Writers Protective Association). It was then that Clara Music realized that there had never been a formal signing and that they didn't really own the rights. When they approached me to sign a formal contract, I said that I would sign only a "Song Writers Guild" contract. They agreed, not really having any choice.

The main feature of the Song Writers Guild contract was that it would expire after 28 years according to the United States copyright law and the copyright would revert to the writer, who could then negotiate a renewal for the next 28 years with the publisher of his choice—usually with a signing bonus if the catalogue had been successful, as mine was.

In the years after World War II, recording became the dominant source of money in the music business. Performers went on national and international tours sometimes just breaking even, or worse—just to promote sales of their LP albums, which now were being sold in the millions. (Michael Jackson's "Thriller" in the 1980s is the champ with sales estimated as high as 60 million worldwide.) It soon became apparent that the biggest long-term money in the business was in publishing this music, because royalties extended for the length of the copyright, which in 1976 was extended to 75 years. (But the 1976 law has since been amended several times to protect copyrights further.) Realizing this, many artists became their own publishers and built their own publishing empires. Some performing artists, because they controlled what song they would or would not sing (a conflict of interest), also demanded half of the writer's share. Many songwriters acquiesced, reasoning that it was better to get half of something from a star on a record than all of nothing by giving the song to an untried performer.

But, through the persistence of the writers and the Song Writers Guild, this practice was diminished. In fact, as music publishing became a bigger piece of the business, and as the volume of activity grew, it became commonplace for a publisher to offer a writer the writer's share and half of the publisher's share of a good catalog. (Herb Alpert of "Tijuana Brass," a few years ago, sold his company, A&M Records, for a reported $500 million. And Michael Jackson, the pop star, recently sold part of his music publishing empire originally valued at $47.5 million in 1985 and now is worth as much as $1 billion.)

In 1956, Harry went on a sort of concert tour with a show called *Sing Man Sing*. I wrote the song "Eden Was Like This" with music by me and lyrics by me and Jay Richard Kennedy, Harry's partner. My other song in this show was called "Lead Man Holler," a work song. ("Lead Man Holler" was not used until the next year in the film *Island in the Sun*.)

This was February 1956 and the release date on the coming *Calypso* album was not until June. I asked for an advance of $2,000, and Kennedy granted it. Page and I had been keeping in touch. We were becoming more than friends. I invited her to my mother's apartment for dinner on New Year's Eve and presented her with a modest ring and proposed. We set the wedding date for May, on Mother's Day.

The *Sing Man Sing* show was not at all well received by the critics; in fact the show was a dog, but Harry's name was rising and it still drew an audience. Everyone was high on the forthcoming *Calypso* album and RCA's enthusiastic prediction of a sale of 300,000 albums turned out to be modest.

A few days before Mother's Day, Page went down to Richmond to prepare for our wedding. My brother drove me down the day before, and we were married at Fifth Street Baptist Church where Page had grown up. Her aunt and uncle had raised her after her mother died when Page was three, and her father deserted the family. She had gone to Sunday school, Girl Scouts and had received a scholarship from the church to attend Virginia Union University and its seminary. She was Miss Armstrong at Armstrong High, and Miss Union at Virginia Union, and she had represented Richmond in various projects in high school and in college.

My brother was best man and my sister, mother, and father came down from New York. It was a warm, beautiful day, and the large church was full that Sunday morning. We were married at the end of the morning service. The minister was proud of Page and spoke to me privately afterwards.

There had always been stories about the vagaries of show business and particularly the struggles and exploitation of blacks in the media—and naturally some were a bit apprehensive about me. The people of Richmond told me to take good care of their girl, and I promised I would. There was a reception after the service. My father's gift was a check for $1,000, which was prominently displayed among the gifts (my father had just received the money as part of a settlement in an automobile accident).

That evening my brother and his wife drove us back to New York where we spent our first night together at the Hotel New Yorker. The next day we left for a few days honeymoon at our friend Bruno Aron's Festival House resort in Lenox, Mass.

Darryl Zanuck, the head of production at 20th Century Fox Studios, was leaving Fox to start an independent company. His first production was to be a movie based on the book by the English writer Alec Waugh titled *Island in the Sun*. It was a story set in the British West Indies, where the emerging black population was growing politically and mixing with their former rulers, and the intrigue and interracial affairs that it set off. The situation of racial mixing in the Caribbean in many ways reflected the social upheaval that was going on in the US in the early 1950s, the early days of the Civil Rights movement.

The 1950s was an era of much more mixing of the races, especially in such urban centers as New York and Chicago, where interracial dating became "legitimate." For instance, there was a noticeable leaning of some of the most successful black actors and singers toward marrying white women; this did not set well with many black women, who were up in arms about it. This was particularly taken up by black female writers who expressed their indignation by writing such pieces as Ntozake Shange's *For Colored Girls Who've Considered Suicide When the Rainbow is Enuf* and Aretha Franklin's hit song "I Will Survive." The fact is that all of these marriages were to relatively ordinary women, as none of the really big stars would be romantically linked to black men at that time. (Which still persists.) On the other hand, several black female personalities began to tie the knot with lesser known whites. Well, it was a start!? I sometimes wondered whether it would have changed the perception of the black family if these same black personalities had married blacks.

Zanuck chose Harry Belafonte as the male lead. He had starred in *Carmen Jones* the year before. Joan Fontaine, a renowned white movie star was to play opposite him (although she was somewhat older than Belafonte). James Mason, Dorothy Dandridge, Michael Rennie and Joan Collins also were featured in the movie.

Controversy arose because it was the first time that a black and white star were linked romantically in a major motion picture. The South threatened a boycott, and the KKK threatened to burn down theatres. Zanuck countered by saying that he planned to distribute the film internationally. Harry's office got in touch with me and asked if I would collaborate with Harry on writing the songs to be featured in the film. Just about this time the *Calypso* album was released and went to the top of the charts. It was being played everywhere, especially the songs "Jamaica Farewell" and "Day-O." I owned eight of the eleven songs in the album.

After the amazing success of the Belafonte *Calypso* album, things began to happen. I received what would be today's equivalent of over one million dollars in royalties, during the first year of release (1956-7). I could sense an artistic maturing which began with my early growing up in a poor family in Brooklyn. I had lived in ghettos and gone through the public school system. I had experienced both overt and subtle discrimination. I went to war across the seas, on the other side of the world in the army, where I started my serious studies. There I lived among diverse peoples. I returned home to the United States and studied at some of the best colleges in different parts of the country under the GI Bill. I lived in New York, Tucson, Chicago, and Los Angeles during the development stages of the civil rights movement, where I played my part. I was fairly well read and was involved in the cultural and creative life of the city. I had begun to realize what I had accomplished, and to see the world in a broader perspective. I absorbed the cultural and ethnic differences of various people, and also the underlying sameness of many seemingly diverse peoples. I had become a man of ideas, possibilities, and hope. I felt I had hit my stride, and possessed more confidence in attaining my goals. I had evolved into a man of some means, with a budding family, and I was beginning at age 32 to enjoy the "sweet smell of success."

As a person of West Indian and American descent, I was keenly interested in the move toward independence in the Caribbean in the mid-1950s as well as the civil rights movement in the US. To me they were definitely related, so I approached the movie assignment with as much passion as I could muster. Writing for the film was exactly what I wanted at the time, and I felt eminently qualified for the task. But I was a little unsure of what they meant by collaboration, since I did not consider Harry my collaborator (in the true sense of the term) in the *Calypso* album, or the show *Sing Man Sing*.

Harry and I arranged to meet to discuss the movie, the plot, and his character. I went home and returned a few days later with a song entitled "O Sunlit Island." Harry liked my work and suggested I add another verse, which I did. We met again and Will Lorin, Harry's musical director, suggested I change the song's title from "O Sunlit Island" to "Island in the Sun." I agreed.

They had also chosen another song for the movie, a work song called "Lead Man Holler," which I had written for the *Sing Man Sing* show the previous winter that hadn't been put into that show. This song fit the movie very well as written, in a waterfront scene with Joan Fontaine and local fishermen.

I took on the task of expressing the aspirations of the Caribbean people in the title song of the movie, which was graphically depicted at the beginning of the film during the titles, with Belafonte and chorus singing the title song against a backdrop of beautiful scenes of the island.

Caribbean Assembly Programs in the public schools (1973-80)

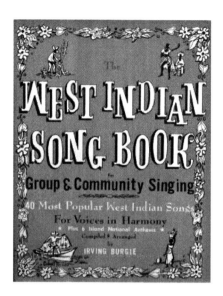

Published *West Indian Song Book* (1973)

Campaign Poster

At the Harlem Writers Guild bash at the Burgie home: (left to right) Jean Carey Bond, Burgie, Bill Tatum, Loften Mitchell, Alice Childress, Bill Ford, Sara Wright Kaye, John Henrik Clarke and John O. Killens, the president and author of the novels *Youngblood* and *Black Man's Burden*

With the "Mighty Sparrow" Barbados ('85).
Sparrow is billed as the "Calypso King of the World".

Dr. Julian Garvey, son of Marcus Garvey; Archie Spigner,
City Councilman from Queens; Page Burgie; and Prof. John Henrik
Clarke, the African historian at a reception in Professor Clarke's honor

Ballad for Bimshire (1963)

C.P.R Voter Registration Drive (1969)

With New York City Mayor John V. Lindsay (1970)

C.P.R. Reception for U.S. Congresswoman Shirley
Chisholm (Actress Ruby Dee at left)

Receiving plaque from actress Dina Merrill at the Songwriters Hall of
Fame for his songs selling over one hundred million records (1983)

Awarded honorary Doctor of Letters degree from
the University of the West Indies (1989)

The movie *Beetlejuice* (1989)

His songs "The Seine," "El Matador," and
"The Wanderer" were recorded by the Kingston Trio.

The new Caribbean musical for children

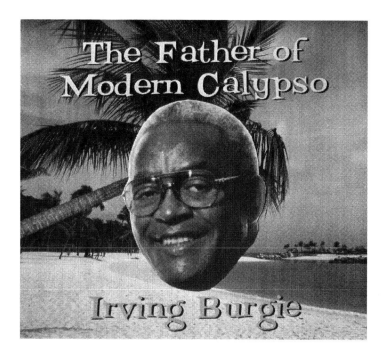

Burgie's new Valley Entertainment CD

Mr. and Mrs. Irving Burgie

Queen Mary 2~August 2005

## ISLAND IN THE SUN

by Irving Burgie

1.   This is my island in the sun
     Where my people have toiled since time began
     I may sail on many a sea
     Her shores will always be home to me.

Chorus:

     O island in the sun
     Willed to me by my father's hand
     All my days, I will sing in praise
     Of your forests, waters, your shining sand.

2.   When morning breaks the heav'n on high
     I lift my heavy load to the sky
     Sun comes down with a burning glow
     That mingles my sweat with the earth below.

3.   I see woman on bended knee
     Cutting cane for her family
     I see man at the waterside
     Casting nets at the surging tide.

4.   I hope the day will never come
     That I can't awake to the sound of drum
     Never let me miss carnival
     With calypso songs philosophical.

Chorus:

     O island in the sun
     Willed to me by my father's hand

All my days, I will sing in praise
Of your forests, waters, your shining sand.

Shari Music Publishers, the company then jointly owned by
Kennedy and Belafonte, asked for 50 percent of the writer's share of the
*two* songs. This had become a rather common practice in the industry
since the early 1950s when artists began controlling and building their
own publishing houses (which encouraged a conflict of interest). It also
seemed that 20th Century Fox was under the impression that Belafonte
and not Irving Burgie had written the two songs.

In their pre-release publicity and press kits, the studio made no
mention of my name and specifically listed Belafonte as composer
of the songs for the film. When the movie was released, there was no
mention of the songs in the credits on screen or the name of the author
of the songs. All the critics' reviews of the movie, following the press
release supplied by Fox, listed Belafonte as the author of the songs.
Besides Harry Belafonte's obvious attributes as an immensely popular,
handsome, sexy singer, they were also now trying to build him as some
sort of creative genius, who also wrote his own songs. The lead article
in the Fox publicity brochure was headlined "BELAFONTE MOST
GIFTED, DEDICATED OF ARTISTS." This was projected to build
Harry's larger-than-life image towards the film's success.

I am a creative writer who has enjoyed much success. The
songs in the film *Island in the Sun* are top drawer material, created
through my skill and are among my best work. I feel wronged by any
misinterpretation of my authorship.

Shortly after the success of the *Calypso* album, Belafonte and I
met to discuss a new treatment for a song, "Mary's Little Boy Child,"
which had been recorded a few years before by "Leonard DePaur
and His Infantry Chorus." It had a happy jump up calypso rhythm.
Belafonte wanted to include the song in a Christmas program for the

British Broadcasting Corporation (BBC). Harry, Will Lorin, his musical director, and I met in the studio apartment of Harry's guitarist, Millard Thomas. They told me they wanted the song to sound like a slow Christmas ballad. Millard's studio was rather small and they locked me in the bathroom and told me to work on the song while they were working on something else. After about an hour, I emerged from the bathroom with the words and new chorus for "Mary's Little Boy Child." They were very happy with it, and when it was presented on Belafonte's BBC Christmas special in England, it was a huge hit. It was also a big Christmas hit in the U.S.A and abroad, and since then, has been heard round the world as a standard during the Christmas season.

### Mary's Boy Child (chorus)

Hark now hear the angels sing,
New king born today,
And man will live forever more
Because of Christmas Day.
Trumpets sound and angels sing,
Listen what they say:
That man will live forever more
Because of Christmas Day.

A couple of years earlier, my father was hit by a car and suffered compound fractures of both legs. It was agreed that my mother would take him home again and nurse him back to health while the court case was pending. My father never really had a nickel left over in his life, but at the trial his lawyers dwelt on the accomplishments of his children, my brother, a lieutenant in the army, my sister, a secretary in the housing authority in Washington, and my budding career as a musician-singer-writer. The jury was obviously impressed. My father was awarded a $50,000 settlement, which left him with about $35,000 after legal fees. This was an enormous sum of money to poor people. We went house hunting, and my father paid down $10,000 on a house in St. Albans, Queens. The closing on the house was set for October 30, 1956.

Just before Page and I married, we answered an ad for a furnished apartment from an elderly couple in the *Amsterdam News*, a black weekly. We went up to the top of the Bronx to see the apartment and rented it for six months while the couple would be in New Jersey working. We moved in right after our return from our honeymoon. We were still watching our money; the royalties wouldn't start coming until December. (We had no idea how much we would receive.)

That October my mother and father moved into their new home in St. Albans. It was the first house we had ever lived in. Mom and Dad occupied the ground floor. Page and I had a small but comfortable apartment upstairs, and my sister transferred from Washington and took the small apartment in the basement with her husband and son. Page was pregnant and expecting a child in March. But after we returned from Lenox, Page went right to work helping prepare the summer season at Camp Minisink. She worked out of the Minisink Town House in Harlem.

With the amazing success of the *Calypso* album, I was busy getting material and ideas ready for the next album. Harry and I would get together fairly often to discuss the new album, which was slated for the next year (1958). I was invited to celebrity-filled parties at Harry's apartment on West End Avenue from time to time, and we were friendly, but we really weren't very tight socially—which seemed to work just fine.

Page spent the summer at Camp Minisink as a head counselor and I went up to visit her on weekends. I spent some days at Tanglewood and did some fireside concerts at Festival House. The second Belafonte album of my songs titled *Belafonte Sings of the Caribbean* was in the works and included "Island in the Sun" and "Lead Man Holler" from the film. "Angelina" was also among the ten songs set for the new LP. The album was released in 1958 around the time of the release of the film *Island in the Sun*.

Also in the same Belafonte album was a song entitled "Don't Ever Love Me." The chorus melody was my reworking of a song originally from Haiti called "Choucounne," which I had traced back to 1875. My version was the first time that this melody was used in a pop song. Seven months later, the melody was picked up by Norman Luboff, the choral director, who had worked on the Belafonte album. He called his version "Yellow Bird" and it was first sung by The Mills Brothers and became immensely popular. I also later recorded a new lyric for the song for a children's play for McGraw Hill Publishing Company.

We spent the winter furnishing our apartment and settling into the house. Mom was quite happy to be in a house, and I gave my father driving lessons and he bought a brand new Chevrolet. He was 60 years old. The house in St. Albans was not far from the Adesleigh Park section, which had attracted such black luminaries as Jackie Robinson, Roy Campanella, Count Basie and Billie Holliday in the late 1940s. Blacks were rapidly taking over the entire area, and whites were victims of "blockbusting," a tactic used by white real estate brokers to prod the whites out. It had been a predominantly middle-class German community.

When I started writing for Harry, he had just changed managers. His first manager was Jack Rollins, and then Richard Kennedy came on. Kennedy was introduced to me as Harry's manager and partner. He was also a partner in Belafonte's developing publishing houses, Shari and Clara Music. A short while after "Island in the Sun," there was a falling-out between Harry and Kennedy. After that, Harry became his own manager and hired Phil Stein to handle the day-to-day business, of which publishing was one aspect.

In the meantime, Belafonte's popularity soared. That summer he
was invited to appear with the New York Philharmonic Orchestra at
Lewisohn Stadium in a special concert (an unusual step). The stadium
is uptown near City College, and the traffic jam that the concert
created was so great that Belafonte was half an hour late getting to
the stadium.

The development of calypso and other ethnic popular music in
the Caribbean islands was inhibited by one major factor: the aspiring
songwriter simply couldn't make much money because the market,
particularly in the English-speaking islands, was too small. The
record and publishing business could rarely produce enough of a
royalty to justify the effort of composing music and lyrics for a song.
That left songwriting to unsophisticated locals who created most of the
double-entendre calypsos that were popular at the time. The songs were
bawdy, naughty, and often good for a laugh, but only made money for
the local record companies. Each singer operated independently and
was usually given $50 for recording a song, for which he also signed
over the copyright. Local singers gained popularity from the sale of
these records and attracted fans to the night spots where they worked,
where their records were for sale after the show.

The most successful of those performers, the "Mighty Sparrow,"
was the most popular calypsonian in the islands and made a fairly good
living there; he was also popular with West Indian communities in New
York, Toronto, London, and Brooklyn where he often appeared. Other
leading calypsonians were Lord Invader, Duke of Iron, King Radio,
Attila the Hun and Lord Melody.

Calypso was centered around the carnival in Trinidad that took
place the weekend before Ash Wednesday, the beginning of Lent.
The King of Calypso was chosen and received prizes (sometimes a
new car) and a cash award of as much as $25,000. The new songs
were the rage for the season, and the next year there would be another

crop of songs vying for the prize. Until Belafonte's *Calypso* album in 1956, calypso was not a recognized category in American pop music. In the Caribbean, the carnival itself was a mostly black affair, but the carnival queen, in a different ceremony, was selected by the Chamber of Commerce and was always white. This persisted until the dawn of Independence in the early 1960s.

Life was a struggle for the majority of West Indians for most of the year, but everything came together for the costumed bands, parades, revelry, dance, and general organized mayhem of Carnival Weekend.

As tourism grew in the Caribbean in the 1950s and especially in the 1960s after Cuba was closed to American tourists, each island developed its own singers on the style of the Trinidad calypsonian to perform in the resorts and clubs. Some islands developed their own carnival, but none on the scale of Trinidad. The steel band, with instruments made from oil drums in Trinidad during World War II, spread to all the other islands, to the extent that the US Navy organized its own steel band to tour the world.

As independence approached, many islands opened their high schools to all qualified students, and the University of the West Indies opened its first campus in Kingston, Jamaica, in 1948 as the University College of the West Indies.

Rhythm and dance, with its African roots, were strong elements in the culture of the Caribbean. Katherine Dunham, the black American dancer, choreographer, and anthropologist, wrote her dissertation on the development of the Caribbean idiom in two books, *Journey to Accompong*, which dealt with her work with the Maroons in the high mountain regions of Jamaica and *Island Possessed*, a book on the folklore, dance, and rituals of Haiti. She created an international sensation in concerts and night clubs with her Caribbean revues, and her Dunham Method became the model of Caribbean dance as taught by her disciples: Lavinia Williams, Savilla Forte, Tally Beatty, Alvin Ailey and Jean Léon Destiné. Limbo, shango, fire dance and several ritual dances became standard fare in the shows at all resorts in the Caribbean.

Little cafes sprang up in New York City with calypso-style dancers in costume teaching the steps to customers. The airlines began developing the Caribbean into a major tourist destination, and tourism gradually replaced sugar cane and bananas as the major source of income in the islands. Many musicians and singers in the islands learned the Belafonte repertoire and sang it to the tourists. (This practice has persisted to this day.) The *Calypso* album was No. 1 on the Billboard charts for thirty-two weeks and remained in the top 100 for ninety-nine weeks. The album caught the music industry by complete surprise, and they had no artists or catalogue to compete with it.

Consequently the burgeoning popular song industry in the US in the1950s was stalled. Calypso had temporarily derailed rock and roll, and the industry was in disarray. Until this time, adults had controlled the music and record-buying industry. With the coming of rock and roll, the younger generation, led by Elvis Presley, was rapidly taking over the music business. Calypso found a niche in the folk movement, which was still building and grew to a high point with the Kingston Trio and Bob Dylan. By then the newly developing artists, realizing the value of publishing, started their own publishing houses or became co-publishers of their songs with major publishing houses, who managed and exploited their catalog.

# Solfa 8

*do*

IN MARCH 1957, my son Irving Jr. was born; Page retired from the City Mission Society to become a full-time mother and homemaker. With royalty money pouring in, I began to make plans. When Irving Jr. was six months old, we left for a one-month stay in the Blue Mountains of Jamaica, a few miles from Kingston, the capital, in a place called Irish Town. Halfway up the mountain we passed the road to Gordon Town where Louise Bennett lived, who had been with my group at the Vanguard in 1954. Louise had moved back to Jamaica and established herself.

She lived in a large house with her husband Eric and a cadre of housekeepers. She wrote for the local newspaper and did a popular weekly television show. She starred in the annual pantomime show that was a fixture in Jamaica. She was the best-known personality in Jamaica for many years. She kept alive the Jamaican folklore in dialect prose, verse, public performances, and plays, both in Jamaica and abroad. We met many people and artists in Jamaica through Louise, from the premier, Norman Manley, to the celebrated Frat's Quintet and the choreographer Ivy Baxter. Louise threw a big party for us at her home, and many Jamaican artists were invited, and several performed. I kept my hand in with a little writing while enjoying Jamaica. We returned to New York refreshed and I went house hunting.

After Christmas we left for California to visit Page's aunt in Los Angeles and the new Disneyland in Anaheim. Returning to New York I contacted the travel agent Evelyn Scheyer, and we planned a six-month trip, first class all the way, to Europe, Africa, Scandinavia, and Israel. We took my brother's mother-in-law, Ilda Glenn, along to care for Irving Jr., who was just 11 months old when we left on March 1$^{st}$.

Our itinerary was Lisbon, Portugal; Accra, Ghana; Lagos and Kano, Nigeria; Rome and Capri, Italy; Tel Aviv, Haifa and Jerusalem, Israel; Frankfurt, Dachau and Munich, Germany; Paris, France; Brussels (World's Fair), Belgium; Amsterdam, Holland; Copenhagen, Denmark; Stockholm, Sweden; and London, England.

Just before leaving, I bought a three-bedroom house in Queens, New York, not far from my mother's house. We set the closing date for September 1$^{st}$, the day after our return from abroad.

Irving, Jr. spent his first birthday in Nigeria and the trip was planned to coincide with the first anniversary of independence in Ghana, and the tenth anniversary in Israel. (I had met Shoshana Damari and Yaffa Yarkoni, Israeli entertainers, in the US, and we looked them up in Tel Aviv.) On the trip we stayed at the finest hotels, Bayerischer Hof in Munich, Amstel Hotel in Amsterdam, Savoy Hotel in London. In Paris I rented an apartment for a month's stay near the Bois de Boulogne on the avenue Paul Doumer. One day while in Paris we heard the incessant beeping of car horns and thought it was a wedding, only to learn that it was the dawn of the Fifth Republic. In London we spent the first week at the Savoy Hotel. Then we rented an apartment in Ealing and had an enjoyable stay, even though the Notting Hill riots (a racially motivated neighborhood conflict) were going on at the time. In both Paris and London I rented a car as we spent a little over a month in each place.

All in all, the six-month tour was always interesting and exciting, and we learned a lot. We also brought things for our new home—crystal from Sweden, china from Harrods in London, and artwork from Ghana and Nigeria.

When we returned we moved into our new home. The *Calypso* album of Belafonte was No. 1 in just about every country, with many artists singing the songs in their own language. I was greeted enthusiastically in most places that connected me with the songs. The second album I wrote for Belafonte called *Belafonte Sings of the Caribbean* was released that summer (1958), and it was well received. The movie *Island in the Sun* had come out to mixed reviews from the press, but the film made money and the song "Island in the Sun" was a hit. It also became the unofficial national anthem of most of the West Indian islands. It was one of the biggest hits ever in Germany, as "Wo Meine Sonne Scheint" sung by Caterina Valenti.

Stan Freeburg, a comedian of the time, did a comedy takeoff on Harry Belafonte's recording of "Day-O" that was played for days on practically every music station. Harry had to take "Day-O" out of his act for years. As memory of Freeburg's takeoff faded, Belafonte came back with "Day-O" as strong as ever. Over the past half-century he has become universally identified with the song.

As the confrontations with black civil rights groups like NAACP, CORE, and SNCC intensified, the police in some areas of the south were using tear gas, fire hoses, dogs and clubs against the protesters. The Ku Klux Klan was burning crosses on the lawns of black leaders. A black church was bombed, killing four young black girls. Medgar Evers, the president of the NAACP in Mississippi, was murdered. Michael Schwerner and Andrew Goodman, two white boys from New York, and James Chaney from Mississippi were murdered when they went to Mississippi with a civil rights group to help organize a voter registration drive among blacks.

There emerged a few splinter groups among the civil rights activists that began to think that the NAACP and Martin Luther King's platform of non-violence was wearing thin in the face of the southern police and the Ku Klux Klan, and they advocated arming themselves against armed attackers. Some members of SNCC and CORE, such as Stokely Carmichael and Rap Brown, pioneered this approach, and groups like the Black Panthers, headed by Eldridge Cleaver and Bobby Seale, were involved in shoot-outs with their assailants. There was also major burning and looting in black areas of Los Angeles (Watts), Detroit, Philadelphia, Newark and elsewhere.

Robert Williams, the president of the North Carolina branch of the NAACP, was involved in an exchange of gunfire when members of the KKK attacked the home of a black. In the melee, they were charged with kidnapping two whites whom they were holding for their own safety. With the sheriff and posse in pursuit, Robert Williams escaped and turned up a short while later in Cuba, which had been recently taken over by Fidel Castro. (He later returned to the U.S.) In the long run the tactics of Martin Luther King won out with the March on Washington in 1963.

When we returned from our six-month trip and settled into the house, I joined the NAACP, Jamaica, Queens, branch as a life member. I was asked to become chairman of the Life Membership Committee by the incoming branch president, Dupree White, who was a dynamic, dedicated worker. The Jamaica branch was a particularly active part of the organization. I was also invited to join the Harlem Writers Guild by John O. Killens, its president and author of the novels *Youngblood* and *Black Man's Burden*. It was a workshop that met at different members' houses each week, to read their work. The membership included such budding writers as Rosa Guy, Sylvester Leaks, Sarah Wright, Maya Angelou, John Henrik Clarke, Bill Forde, and Louise Meriwether, who all read their "novels in preparation" at the guild meetings. The guild also discussed many issues of the day as they affected black people.

As a member of the American Society of African Culture, I was asked by its director Ted Harris, to visit the office of the magazine *Presence Africaine* and its editor Alioune Diop, a French writer and intellectual from Senegal who, together with Aimé Cesare from Martinique and Leopold Senghor from Senegal, expounded the term "Negritude." They had been expanding "black" from a feeling of inferiority to a feeling of pride, acceptance and love. They projected Negritude to be the highly positive expression of peoples of the black Diaspora as they existed in the colonies of Africa, south of the Sahara and as they were scattered from Africa, mostly as slaves to South and North America and the Caribbean. The works of black writers were championed on a global basis, especially writers like Claude McKay and Langston Hughes in the US and their counterparts in the Diaspora who vindicated the richness of black culture.

W.E.B. Dubois organized the first Pan-African Congress in 1919. The concept of Negritude continued to develop within the black Diaspora. In 1966, *Presence Africaine* sponsored the first World Wide Festival of Negro Arts in Dakar, Senegal. Members of the Harlem Writers Guild and the Society of African Culture were part of the American team that attended the event.

When I returned from my six-month trip from Europe and Africa, I was asked to join the board of directors of Operation Cross Roads Africa by its director Jim Robinson. In my student days, I had been a counselor at his summer camp ten years before. He had asked me to look up a couple of French-Africans while I was in West Africa and Paris. He had me go on a recruitment tour for Cross Roads that took me to several black colleges in the South, plus a couple of Ivy League campuses. Of course it didn't hurt that I was a composer of well-known popular songs and I did a little songfest with my guitar as part of my presentation.

With the *Calypso* album and the songs in the film *Island in the Sun* to my credit, my reputation as a writer began to grow. While abroad, I was thinking up ideas for songs about the various places we visited. It was 1958, and the Kingston Trio had just surfaced with their big hit "Tom Dooley," an old Appalachian folk song that described in grim detail the saga of a man who stabbed his girlfriend to death and was about to be hanged for his crime.

I got in touch with their publisher and arranged to meet them at the Blue Angel, where they were appearing in New York. I had a song in each of their next three million-selling albums: "The Seine," "El Matador," and "The Wanderer," songs I had written reflecting my six-month trip abroad.

Just about this time many of the newly independent countries of Africa had joined the United Nations and were eager to make their presence felt in the new order, and they sent many delegates to establish consulates and missions in New York. I became affiliated with a group called the American Society of African Culture, which had headquarters in downtown New York, and served to acquaint the American black artistic and cultural community with the newly arrived African delegates, officers, dignitaries, writers and artists. At the United Nations there was a steady flow of lunches, cocktail parties, receptions, and lectures by countries such as Ghana, Nigeria, Sierra Leone, Senegal, and Ethiopia. There was a seminar arranged between the Harlem Writers Guild and the American Society of African Culture that drew many black writers and their African counterparts and was successful.

With the coming of independence to the countries of Africa south of the Sahara, delegates, emissaries, and staff were sent to establish consulates in and around New York City with a focus at the United Nations. (Ghana was the first colony to declare independence in 1957.) Black Americans were eager and proud to establish a dialogue with the Africans and invite them to their homes and functions.

My brother Will was doing a terrific job as director of boys for the New York City Mission Society's Harlem branch, and the cadet corps was growing by leaps and bounds. New chapters were forming, primarily outside of Manhattan and the Bronx. A foundation gave them $3 million to build a new cadet center in the Bronx. The total program now involved thousands of children between the ages of eight and eighteen. I served on the board of the cadet corps for many years.

After 1958 most of my activities were centered on organizational work in the civil rights movement and my creative writing. When I joined the Harlem Writers Guild I was feeling around for my next venture. I had had about two dozen songs published and was doing well. I was thinking about a real challenge, like writing a show. I zeroed in on my mother and decided to do a musical depicting her growing up on a sugar plantation in Barbados. But the story began to shift focus to a fictitious girl of 17 named Daphne Byfield, who became the ingénue of the piece.

In the winter of 1960 I rented a house in Barbados, right by the sea. My wife, son and I spent three months there as I developed the story's music and lyrics and got a good taste of Barbados, its history and lifestyle. Barbados is in the Lesser Antilles, roughly 21 miles long and 14 miles wide with a population of 250,000. In 1960 it was on the verge of joining a federation of English-speaking colonies that included Jamaica, Trinidad, St. Lucia, Antigua, St. Vincent, Grenada, and British Guiana. The project fell through when Jamaica pulled out and declared its own independence in 1962. The other islands declared their independence over the next five years, but remained a part of the British Commonwealth. A sizeable number of East Indians and Chinese were also scattered over the British colonies, mostly in Trinidad and Guyana, usually the descendants of East Indians and Chinese who had arrived as indentured workers to replace the freed slaves when slavery was abolished in the British colonies in 1838. By 1960, tourism was fast replacing sugar as the No. 1 industry in the Caribbean.

Meanwhile the black community all over America was aroused and organized, with marches, protest meetings, boycotts, sit-ins, voter registration, and confrontations. Besides the Ku Klux Klan, the main antagonist was the police in those southern states that were defending their state-imposed discriminatory laws against blacks. All the organizations I belonged to were involved in the civil rights struggle and the tide was swelling. It was a great time to be a black in America. It was a great time to be a white in America. In many ways it was America's finest hour.

After the release of the second album for Harry, *Belafonte Sings of the Caribbean* in 1958, I began work on a third album. When it was near ready I went down to Miami for a couple of weeks to discuss it with Harry, who was working at the Eden Rock Hotel. Harry stayed at the hotel and his musicians stayed at a smaller and less expensive hotel nearby. I stayed with the musicians, as I knew them well. We were not allowed to use the pool, so every day I spent my time away from Harry at the Sir John Hotel, a black hotel across town that had a pool and a friendly atmosphere. I recall that the singer Johnny Ray (Little White Cloud) was one of the nightclub attractions there. The third album for Belafonte was called *Jump Up Calypso*, and I had eight of the twelve songs on the album. My favorites were "Angelina," "Kingston Market," and "Land of the Sea and Sun." By now I had amassed 32 songs with Belafonte since 1955 and the *Calypso* album.

A little later I went to Washington, D.C. where Harry was working on a show in which he was featuring the South African singer Miriam Makeba in her first appearance in the US. Harry arranged a meeting between me and Miriam with the idea of my doing an album for her. I wrote the song "River Come Down," which she recorded in her next album, but we were not able to continue on the project because she was moving around a lot.

Later that fall I took off with Page and Irving Jr. for a trip to Mexico. I rented an apartment on the Reforma in Mexico City for three months.

We brought along a friend who was a retired nurse to take care of Irving Jr. We had letters of introduction to a couple of people and they helped us get started and meet others. We first met Elizabeth Catlett, the black American sculptor. She had married a Mexican and was raising a family in Mexico.

I rented a car and we would spend about a week at the apartment entertaining friends and being entertained, then we would head out for a week or ten days toward Guadalajara, Oaxaca, Vera Cruz, Acapulco, Guanajuato, Taxco and Cuernevaca, stopping off for a day or two at different points of interest on the way and returning to Mexico City. We bought some fine silver items and objets d'art for our house.

We were intrigued by the murals of Orozco and Diego Rivera whose sister we also met. It was a wonderful three months and quite educational. We enjoyed trying out our "college Spanish" whenever we could.

Jim Grant, my lawyer at the time, got me interested in a new black magazine called *The Urbanite*. The first successful black magazine at the time was *Ebony*, and it had been out since shortly after the war. It projected primarily the many "firsts" among blacks in the slowly changing socio-economic scene, and the accomplishments of black celebrities. *The Urbanite* was yet another step up in sophistication, and it was felt that there was room and a need for this kind of content. I was one of the principal backers, and we threw great effort into it, but we were forced to close down after the fifth monthly issue, primarily because of problems in distribution—typical with start-up ventures.

By now I was involved with my musical play *Ballad for Bimshire* (a nickname for Barbados) and read it from time to time at the Harlem Writers Guild. After a year and a half, I took on Loften Mitchell, a fellow writer and acquaintance, to assist me in the writing of the book.

Up to this time there had been only one black play produced on Broadway since the days of the Harlem Renaissance in the 1920s,

and that was Lorraine Hansbury's *Raisin in the Sun* in 1959. It was a
beautiful play and was enthusiastically received. Then followed *Purlie
Victorious*, a satire by Ossie Davis in 1960. The only black subject
musical at that time was *Jamaica* by Harold Arlen and E. Y. Harburg
in 1957 starring Lena Horne. It was a mediocre show, but it ran for
two seasons on the drawing power of its star.

By the spring of 1962, after a three-year effort, *Ballad for Bimshire*
was ready for a reading. I had written the lyrics and music for the
show, and Loften Mitchell and I had collaborated on the book.
Sammy Benskin, a pianist and arranger, was the music director and
arranger. The reading was held at Steinway Hall on West 57th Street.
We presented the songs in concert style with a bit of narration.
Christine Spencer, the soprano, played the part of the ingenue Daphne
Byfield. The reading was well received by the invited audience, and
we began to talk about putting a company together. That summer I
rented a three-bedroom house in Sag Harbor, Long Island, for the
month of July. I worked on the show while there, and invited friends
and co-workers to visit.

My accountant, Bernard Waltzer, became co-producer, and so did
Ossie Davis, who also was featured in the show. Tally Beatty came on
as choreographer, and Ed Cambridge, who had directed off-Broadway,
was the director. Mozelle Forte was the costume designer and Donald
Ryder, the set designer. Sylvester Leaks and Ewart Guinier worked in
promotion and made a special pitch to churches, fraternal groups, and
various organizations in the black community for support. Many people
who had never gone to the theater before got behind us. In effect, it
became an expression of the civil rights movement.

We organized a company for the show, and we offered shares at
$360 each (people could also buy quarter shares at $90 apiece). We
went to several parties at the homes of middle—and upper-class whites
on Long Island and Westchester County and presented mini-shows to
sell shares. Bernie Waltzer was especially helpful in this. We got a

company manager and were able to secure the Mayfair Theater on West 46th Street and Broadway for the production. (It had been Billy Rose's Diamond Horseshoe nightclub, and it was small enough to qualify as off-Broadway.) Equity rules called for a four-week rehearsal schedule for off-Broadway, and we were kept busy with the myriad problems that go with putting on a show.

During our rehearsals, the biggest piece of civil rights legislation was pending before the president and Congress, and all the civil rights organizations, liberal organizations, black and white, the NAACP, CORE, SNCC, labor unions, and churches got together and planned a march on Washington for August 1963 in support of this legislation. Ralph Abernathy, Martin Luther King Jr., James Farmer, and A. Philip Randolph, were the principal speakers in front of the Washington Monument. Hundreds of buses converged on Washington and every available train and mode of transportation was booked. Bayard Rustin, a long-time civil rights advocate, was one of the principal logisticians. The entire cast of my show was given the weekend off to go to Washington. We were all there, from North, South, East, and West. They had predicted a crowd of 150,000. It was a beautiful day and 250,000 people showed up. It was a colorful, orderly, emotion-filled day, as brothers and sisters embraced from coast to coast. Martin Luther King Jr. delivered his famous "I Have A Dream" speech to the multitude of cheering participants.

The next Monday we were back in rehearsal. We had auditioned a talented chorus of singers and dancers, and Tally Beatty was an excellent choreographer. A tremendous spirit of cooperation came from every member of the cast. Things went reasonably well and to top it off, we had to go down to the Tombs (the Manhattan jail) the morning of our first previews to get one of our featured actors, Bobby Hooks, out of jail. (He had been arrested the night before in a scuffle with a taxi driver who refused to pick him up.)

The show opened in mid-October, and on opening night, all those quarter-share backers came out in their finery along with everybody else. It was a real salt-and-pepper audience representing many groups and organizations in the city. In fact, we had to have three opening nights to accommodate everybody. (My wife had to get three new dresses.) Lorraine Hansbury came opening night and also gave us an endorsement. Josephine Baker was in New York and was in the audience. The widow of Medgar Evers was also present, as was Sidney Poitier. We had a cast party at a restaurant across the street to wait for the reviews, which were generally good. Howard Taubman of *The New York Times* said, "Mr. Burgie's songs almost cover the gamut; they are sweet, nostalgic, torch, comic, and ebullient. His lyrics vary in quality from indifferent to joyously apt, but he is rarely shy of an engaging melody and he can unleash rhythms that provide almost as much thrust to the production numbers as a booster rocket on a launching pad."

We were in an off-Broadway house and the cast pay was very low, but the actors and dancers went out and did a fine job. Eight shows a week. We didn't have much money for ads, but the word of mouth was good and we struggled on. We also managed to get the first black cashier, John Grey, into the union and he was the cashier for our show. Sylvester Leaks and Ewart Guinier made the rounds in the black community, setting up theater parties and spreading the word. Four weeks after our show opened, President Kennedy was assassinated on November 22$^{nd}$, 1963. Everything seemed to come to a standstill. The country was in shock, then in mourning. The theater practically died as the two-year-old Kennedy baby stood in salute as his father's bier passed by.

Charles Boyer and Claudette Colbert's hit comedy had to close. Our show put up the closing notice too, and closed two weeks later.

The civil rights movement was moving along on all fronts as a result of the March on Washington, and Martin Luther King Jr. was planning marches in the Deep South. The focus was to change the existing laws that discriminated against blacks, so that the same police and National Guard that attacked us would now defend us. It was as simple as that.

I spent most of my time during this period involved in various organizations participating in the struggle. All over the country the cry could be heard: "We shall overcome." I was collecting enough money in royalties that now came in bits and pieces from all over the world to support my family, so I kept going. I was studying guitar with Franz Casseus, the Haitian guitarist, and preparing a nightclub act, which I unveiled at the Café Au Go Go in the village. I also took a course in writing for the theater and films at the New School and used my show *Ballad for Bimshire* as my vehicle.

Eight years after Irving Jr. our second son, Andrew, was born. Irving Jr. went to a progressive school in Forest Hills that was about 15 percent black. He enjoyed a well-rounded, somewhat privileged education. Page was a good mother and was responsible for his daily coming and going, and we both participated in his educational and social upbringing. He was a healthy, handsome, agile child who did well in his studies. Page served on the board of his nursery, grammar school and high school. (She did the same for Andrew.)

On the morning of June 10, 1964, after Senator Robert Byrd completed a 14-hour and-thirteen-minute address in a filibuster against the Civil Rights Act of 1964, Senator Hubert Humphrey, the bill's manager, concluded that he had the 67 votes required to end the debate. The Civil Rights Act provided protection of voting rights; banned discrimination in public facilities—including private businesses offering public service, such as lunch counters, hotels and theatres; and established equal employment opportunity as the law of the land. (Earlier that year, the ratification of the 24th Amendment had outlawed the poll tax.)

Senator Everett Dirksen, speaking on the floor of Congress that day said, "Stronger than all the armies is an idea whose time has come." He continued, "The time has come for equality of opportunity in sharing in government, in education, and in employment. It will not be stayed or denied. It is here!"

In 1964 Martin Luther King Jr. won the Nobel Peace Prize. He was also prominent in the marches on Montgomery and Selma in Alabama in 1964 and 1965. By 1969, 61 percent of voting-age blacks in America were registered compared to 23 percent in 1964. The Selma-Montgomery marches clearly showed both how far black Americans had come and how far they still had to go. Ten years earlier, blacks had asked if they could sit in the front of the bus; now they were demanding their full rights as Americans. We still faced strong, sometimes violent, opposition but we were further along than we had ever been.

Since 1960, I had been winter vacationing in Barbados every two years. I had some of my mother's side of the family still living there, and I was also something of a celebrity—having written the *Calypso* album for Belafonte. The songs were now popular worldwide. I had also written the music for the songs in the film *Island in the Sun*, which was filmed in Barbados and Grenada. And my show *Ballad for Bimshire* was set in Barbados.

While in Barbados in the winter of 1966, I was asked by some prominent citizens to write the words for their national anthem. They supplied me with a melody that was submitted by Roland Edwards, a music teacher in Speightstown, Barbados. Within the next month I completed the words and had a singer put the anthem on tape, and I sent it to the committee. I was later informed that the government had established a competition for the anthem, the flag, and the coat of arms, among other symbols of sovereignty.

I had gone back to working on various other projects when, in October, I was notified that my lyrics had been selected to be the words of the Barbados National Anthem. In the notice were also two round-trip tickets, hotel accommodations, and an itinerary for Independence Week, which covered a host of gala affairs. There was also a prize of $500 to be given. It was quite an honor to have been chosen—especially for my relatives living in Barbados.

There was a big downpour on the evening of independence but it did not dampen the spirits of the huge crowd at the Savannah where, amid speeches, parades, and patriotic displays, the Union Jack was lowered and the Barbados flag was raised for the first time. All official and semi-official gatherings in Barbados begin with the singing or playing of the National Anthem. It's the first thing in the morning on Radio Barbados and the last thing at night. All schools begin the day with the National Anthem.

In 1967 I recorded an album of my songs for Buddha Records, and in 1968 I had a concert at Carnegie Hall, which was a success thanks to the support of many organizations and schools for whom I had performed over the years.

During the 1960s and 1970s my home was the scene of many receptions for personalities such as Amy Ashwood Garvey, the first wife of Marcus Garvey and co-founder of the UNIA (United Negro Improvement Association); Paul O'Dwyer, president of the New York City Council; Daisy Bates, who led the children into Little Rock Central High School in 1957; and book parties for the authors Rosa Guy (*Bird at My Window*), John O. Killens (*Youngblood*), Louise Meriwether (*Daddy Was a Number Runner*), John H. Clarke (*Garvey and Garveyism*), Maya Angelou (*I Know Why the Caged Bird Sings*), Julian Mayfield (*Grand Parade*), Sarah Wright (*This Child's Gonna Live*) and others.

As a result of the new civil rights legislation, black communities all over began to re-assess their positions and move forward. Basic emphasis was put on voter registration, as most black communities were without black representation, even in local government.

Page and I had been among the first black families to move into our section of Hollis, and the area began changing fast. Dissatisfied with the progress of the political structure in Queens, we and some friends organized a group called the Coalition for Political Representation in southeast Queens. I became its first president, and my house was headquarters for the organization during its first year.

In 1944 Adam Clayton Powell Jr. had been elected to the US Congress. Hulan Jack was the first black borough president of Manhattan in 1953. Bertram Baker was the first black state assemblyman as the choice of the black Democratic club in Brooklyn. Tommy Jones was the next black elected to the assembly from Brooklyn. Next time around he accepted a judgeship, and was replaced by the flamboyant Shirley Chisholm. Shirley became the first black elected to Congress from Brooklyn in 1968. (She later ran for president in the Democratic primary.)

In my area of Queens, we had by the mid-1960s only one black elected official, Ken Brown, a state assemblyman, and southeast Queens was fast becoming one of the most affluent black communities in the country.

Our first project in the CPR was voter registration, which was also the priority of most black organizations. We mapped out the district and began a campaign of doorbell ringing, telephone calls, and demonstrations in front of supermarkets. At the same time in 1968 the New York City teachers called a strike over community control of the public schools. Community volunteers picketed the schools and took over several schools at night, and our coalition members got a good hands-on experience in bringing their bed-rolls and sleeping in the schools on the midnight watches.

We held a successful "youth in action" concert that featured my brother's Cadet Corps in one of the neighborhood school auditoriums. Also there was a dance at the St. Albans Plaza with the actor Ossie Davis as master of ceremonies. In housing, voter registration and schools, the implementation of the civil rights legislation of the 1960s was a formidable challenge then, and it still is.

In 1969, BWIA, the airline of the West Indies, offered me a position in New York as Community Relations Officer, to be a liaison to the community at large. I organized a chorus of close to 100 voices under the auspices of Caribbean House, an organization of West Indians from the islands and countries of the Caribbean. We held weekly rehearsals at St. Peter Claver's church gymnasium. I arranged some of my songs and some folk songs from the various islands and countries (Guyana and Suriname are located in South America), and the chorus grew into a fine performing group. We were invited to sing on various programs, and we ended the season with a full concert at the Brooklyn Academy of Music.

That summer I was invited to rehearse and present a program of my songs with the Lucayan Chorale of Nassau, Bahamas. I spent a month there on Paradise Island rehearsing the Chorale. The performance took place at the new Casino. I brought down Christine Spencer, the soprano, from New York as guest soloist. Scenes from my original *Ballad for Bimshire* were also on the program. Dr. Doris Johnson, a college friend of my wife Page, and who had originally catalogued my home library, was now a senator (the first woman) in the new Pindling government. I also presented a similar show a little later in Antigua and in Barbados using local choruses.

By working primarily out of my home-office, I was able to be on hand and play a role in the raising of my two boys, Andrew and Irving Jr. who went to the same schools, the Queens School, Highland School, Yale University, class of 1978 and 1987. Irving Jr. got his master's at the California Institute of Arts (in film) and Andrew at Hunter College, New York (in environmental health).

During the second year of the Coalition for Political Representation (CPR) I was put up as a candidate in the Democratic primary for the state assembly. We moved our headquarters from my house to a storefront on Farmers Blvd. There we got involved with the ins and outs of getting petitions signed door-to-door. We passed out leaflets, and posted placards, and created a feeling of involvement in the community at large. It was a heavily Democratic area, and the regulars were entrenched. We didn't win the primary but all in all, in terms of community involvement, it was worth the effort—more and more blacks began to seek public office. In the early 1970s, I was a founding member of the United Black Men of Queens, a community service organization that still operates in southeast Queens.

Kingston, Jamaica, has been a leading source of pop music since 1960, having pioneered "Rocksteady," "Ska," and "Reggae" in rapid succession up to the 1970s. The hip-hop music that has been in vogue among the younger generation in the U S for the past 25 years was pioneered in Queens by the group Run DMC. They operated out of Hollis, New York—home to many West Indian families. But the roots of hip-hop, that is, the singing of rhymes to music, were first established in Jamaica in the late 1960s. It was called "Toasting" and later "Dancehall" as sung by such personalities as "U-Roy," "King Sporty," and particularly "Yellowman" (he was a Jamaican albino). Yellowman's recordings were popular in West Indian communities in Brooklyn and Queens. From its introduction by Run DMC, hip-hop has spread around the world and is now the leading pop-music form.

Having been involved with West Indian folklore and music now for many years, and with the experience of leading various choruses and arranging for voices, I began to think of creating a song book. There had been no previous books on West Indian songs available prior to this. *The West Indian Song Book* was produced by a Jamaican friend, who was a printer in Glen Cove. Cabell Turner, Page's brother, a talented illustrator, did the artwork.

When the book was completed I went on a tour from Guyana to the Bahamas to introduce and promote the book. I got the idea of organizing a "Caribbean Day" assembly program to be presented in the public schools. As the composer of the *Calypso* album for Belafonte and of the song "Island in the Sun," and as writer of the book, lyrics and music for *Ballad for Bimshire*, I was successful in arranging interviews with principals in schools all over the City of New York and its environs.

With *The West Indian Song Book* as the focus, I devised a program that included me and Vivia Heron from Jamaica. She had been my secretary with the choral groups and my assistant, and was a capable dancer.

With my guitar, I led the students in pre-rehearsed songs from the song books. Vivia was dressed in a Caribbean costume. We presented a slide show of scenes of the islands—the beaches, the markets, street cries, the people, flora and fauna. The show climaxed with Vivia on stage leading volunteers from the audience in various dances from the islands that ended in high spirits. The principal and the students generally loved the show and in many cases we came back from year to year. The book was put on the New York State approved book list (NYSTL) and was part of the package, together with the performance that the schools bought.

I would get up in the morning, pack the car with speakers, amplifier, microphone, guitar, projector and screen, and costume, pick up Vivia, and set off to the selected school. We usually did a performance at 9:30 AM for the younger kids and at 11:15 AM for the others. We averaged about 60 bookings a year throughout New York City, Long Island, Westchester and New Jersey. This went on for seven years—from 1973 to 1980.

After a couple of seasons, I replaced Vivia on the program with other women; she had started Brooklyn College where she majored in English.

She graduated Phi Beta Kappa from Brooklyn College where she also took her master's. She did her doctoral class-work at City University Graduate Center. Over the years Vivia has been associated with my various projects as secretary, assistant to the director and editor. Since 1984 she has been an English teacher in the New York City public schools.

The song book was a successful venture and there was a second printing in 1975.

Belafonte continued to tour and concertize, and his top songs continued to be "Jamaica Farewell," "Day-O," and "Island in the Sun." He was a great salesman and, as a performer, he helped keep my songs before the public for 50 years. "Day-O" was used as the "Wake Up" call for the crew aboard the Atlantis Space Shuttle On January 12, 1997, and was prominent in the *We Are the World* telecast. In 1979 Belafonte made his first tour to Europe in 20 years, and this tour gave the songs another big boost.

In 1982 the 28-year renewals on my copyrights came up and according to the AGAC contract that I signed with my publisher, the songs would revert to me for the next 28 years. Actually, copyright royalties are shared equally between the writer and the publisher. The publisher's basic obligation is to record your songs and pay you 50 percent of all royalties from sheet music sales, recordings, or licenses for commercials. I would now control 100 percent of the writer's share and also 100 percent of the publisher's share.

Just at this time, I received a letter from Milt Okun who had been musical director for Belafonte in the early 1960s. He had become a successful publisher and built Cherry Lane Music, as well as being co-publisher and mentor to John Denver and Peter, Paul and Mary. He was looking for material for a second album featuring Placido Domingo, the opera tenor, teamed with John Denver, the folk singer. They had had a highly successful first album. Milt remembered my songs and asked me if I had anything to submit. In our conversation I told him that my renewals were coming up, and I was shopping around for a publisher.

By then it was fairly common for publishers to offer 50 percent of the publisher's share for a valuable catalog, which mine certainly was. With the writer's share of 50 percent and a co-publisher's share of 25 percent, I would automatically increase the value of my copyrights by 25 percent. As part of the deal, Milt promised me an instrumental recording of my best songs by the Royal Philharmonic Orchestra, to which I was invited the following spring in London. It was a beautiful recording session arranged and conducted by one of England's best, Larry Ashmore. Cherry Lane also gave me a signing bonus of $175,000. All this was negotiated by my attorney Alvin Deutsch.

Cherry Lane immediately began to exploit my catalog, and in about three years my royalties began to increase from ASCAP and commercial licenses. In 1988 my songs were used in the movie *Beetlejuice* and were widely exposed in a television video with Harry Belafonte. This opened the songs to a new generation of listeners, and kids were walking down the street singing "Day-O." During the 1990s my royalties from all sources averaged over half a million dollars a year.

During the 1990s I put together a combo composed of my musical director Eugene Gray on guitar, Preston Vismale on keyboards, Kim Burgie on drums and recorder, Lloyd Robinson on drums, and Tony Ramsey on bass. About once a week I would rent a rehearsal studio and rehearse and arrange several songs. This continued and at one point we were ready to try out the act. We did one show in Nashville and a couple of television shots and we were presented in the "ASCAP Evenings" at Rainbow and Stars at Rockefeller Center in May of 1997. We put together a double CD of these songs after the turn of the century, which has not yet been released. We worked on a variety of international pop favorites: "Volare," "The Minstrel Boy," "La Mer," "C'est Si Bon" (and other French favorites), "Shenandoah" (and other American favorites), and blended them into a program along with our Caribbean songs.

In 1980, I established the Viola Burgie Literary Prize in the secondary schools in Barbados in honor of my mother, and the program has continued until the present. Over the years I have been an avid traveler around the globe—to Europe, Asia, the Middle East and the Far East, visiting Turkey, the Soviet Union, Scandinavia, Japan, Hong Kong, Thailand, Singapore, Australia, New Zealand and Tahiti—dropping in on Brazil for carnival. During the 1990s, I also took several month-long trips to France. I would rent an apartment, going to Paris or Nice or St. Raphael primarily to study French and absorb some of the French cuisine and culture.

Each winter I would vacation in the Caribbean, mostly in Barbados. I always had a project in mind and usually spent a part of the time writing. I started working on my autobiography in the early1980s and worked steadily for a couple of years. I went back to it in 2002.

In 2001, with the 50th anniversary of the Supreme Court decision coming up in 2004, I began thinking of a musical that would consist of several of my hit songs since 1956 and the *Calypso* album, combined with elements of my 1963 musical *Ballad for Bimshire*. After a couple of different approaches, what developed was a show that I call *Day-O*, set in Jamaica. I had a reading of the show at ASCAP in the fall of 2002 and after more work, another reading at ASCAP in June of 2003. After that, I really got into finishing up my autobiography.

"Day-O," the shout first heard round the world in 1956, is now a part of popular culture. It is heard on television shows, in movies, in commercials and as a hometown cheer in sports arenas of all kinds.

This year, 2006, marks the 50th anniversary of the song "Day-O." The Sunshine Awards Committee and Cherry Lane Music have designated "Day-O" as the recipient of the "Song of The Century" Award at a gala celebration in October 2006 in the Grand Ballroom of the Sheraton Hotel in New York City.

The same occasion will mark the 50th anniversary of the Harry Belafonte album *Calypso*, for which I wrote the songs in 1956 and which became the first album of any kind to sell one million albums. This year also marks the 40th anniversary of the Barbados National Anthem for which I wrote the words.

There is no postlude. I am going to hold this last note, this last *do*, as long as I can.

—O—

# About The Author

IRVING BURGIE'S AUTOBIOGRAPHY is set amid a wider social tapestry that depicts the plight, joys and foibles of one black family in pre-war Brooklyn and the broader black struggle leading up to the Civil Rights movement of the 1940s. The pre-war time was followd by his army experiences as a soldier in an all black battalion in the China-Burma-India theatre in World War II, where he first developed a serious interest in music, and studying in general.

After the war, he went to school under the GI Bill and a few years later he made a meteoric rise to the top echelons of the music business as the songwriter who composed the songs "Day-O," "Jamaica Farewell," "Island in the Sun," and "Mary's Boy Child" and some thirty-four songs for Harry Belafonte, and "The Seine" and "El Matador" for the Kingston Trio.

The story of his growing up in Brooklyn, his army career, and his involvement in the Civil Rights movement, his marriage and family and the black struggle to achieve equality is graphically depicted.

His memoir is an inspiring and novel account of one of the most significant eras in American history—it makes you feel proud to be a human being.